European History 1870–1918:
The rise of nationalism

Studymates

25 Key Topics in Business Studies
25 Key Topics in Human Resources
25 Key Topics in Marketing
Accident & Emergency Nursing
British History 1870–1918
Business Organisation
Cultural Studies
English Legal System
European History 1870–1918
European Reformation
GCSE Chemistry
GCSE English
GCSE History: Schools History Project
GCSE Sciences
Genetics
Getting Started in Radio
Hitler and Nazi Germany (3rd edition)
Land Law
Lenin, Stalin and Communist Russia
Macroeconomics
Organic Chemistry
Poems To Live By
Practical Drama & Theatre Arts
Revolutionary Conflicts
Social Anthropology
Social Statistics
Speaking Better French
Speaking English
Studying Chaucer
Studying History
Studying Literature
Studying Poetry
The Changing Nature of Warfare
The New Science Teache
Troubleshoot Your Probl
Understanding Forces
Understanding Maths
Using Information Techi
War Poets 1914–18
Writing an Academic Essay

Many other titles in preparation

European History 1870–1918

The rise of nationalism

Robert Johnson

www.**studymates**.co.uk

First published in 2004 by Studymates Limited, PO Box 2, Bishops Lydeard, Somerset TA3 3YE, United Kingdom

Telephone: (01823) 432002
Fax: (01823) 430097

Typeset by PDQ Typesetting, Newcastle-under-Lyme
Printed and bound in Great Britain by Bell & Bain Ltd, Glasgow

Contents

List of illustrations   viii

Foreword   ix

Preface   xi

1. **Europe in 1870: Nation States, the Capitalist Economy and Society**   **1**
   The European states   1
   European economies and industrialisation   5
   Social classes in Europe   7
   The diplomatic situation in 1870   11
   Tutorial   13

2. **France: From Second Empire to the Third Republic**   **14**
   The Second Empire   14
   The Franco-Prussian War, 1870–71   15
   The Republic: internal threats to stability   16
   Foreign policy   21
   Historical controversies   23
   Tutorial   24

3. **Germany: The Second Reich**   **25**
   The Franco-Prussian War and the unification of Germany   25
   Bismarck, 1871–1890   27
   Wilhelmine Germany, 1890–1914   34
   Revisionist views of German history   41
   Tutorial   41

4. **The Eastern Question**   **43**
   The Ottoman Empire   43
   The Eastern question, 1875–78   44
   The Balkan States and the Bulgarian question, 1885–56   47
   The rise of the Turkish nationalists   50
   Tutorial   52

5. **The Austro-Hungarian Empire**   **53**
   The dual monarchy   53
   Nationalism   55
   Balkan rivalries   57
   Historical controversies   57
   Tutorial   58

6. Russia, 1870–1914   **60**
The Tsarist régime   60
Revolutionary organisations and reaction   65
Economic problems   68
Russia on the eve of revolution   71
Foreign policy   74
Historical controversies   75
Tutorial   76

7. Britain, 1870–1914   **77**
Free trade and industrialisation   77
The British Empire   78
Democratic governments   78
Themes in British foreign policy   83
Historical controversies   83
Tutorial   84

8. Italy, 1870–1914   **86**
The legacy of unification   86
Liberal governments   88
Domestic problems   89
The relations between the state and the Papacy   93
Tutorial   94

9. New Imperialism   **96**
The motives for imperialism   96
The causes of the rivalry between the European powers   99
The partition of Africa   100
Imperialism in Asia   105
The response of the Islamic world   109
Historical controversies   109
Tutorial   110

10. International Relations and the Causes of the First World War, 1870–1914   **112**
The alliance network and the balance of power in 1900   112
Germany's *Weltpolitik*   114
International crises after 1900   115
The Arms Race, 1906–14   117
The Balkan Wars, 1912–13   119
The July Crisis   120
Responsibility for the war   123
Controversies surrounding the causes of the First World War   124
Tutorial   125

11. The Great War, 1914–1918   **127**
The failure to achieve 'quick victories'   127
The Western Front   129
The Eastern Front   133
The other theatres of war   134
The economic effects of the war   135
The Allied victory in 1918   138
The revolutions in Russia in 1917 and in Germany in 1918   138

Historical interpretations of the First World War 141
Tutorial 142

12. Historical Concepts and Conclusions **144**
Concepts in European history 144
Conclusions: The rise of the West 147
Changes in the European economy 147
Changes in European society 148
Changes in political ideas 149
International diplomacy 149
The impact of war 150
European integration and disintegration 150
Tutorial 151

Appendix: Model Answers **153**

Glossary **155**

Useful Web Sites **156**

Bibliography and Further Reading **158**

Index **159**

List of illustrations

1. Europe in 1870   11
2. Germany in 1870   26
3. The Balkans in 1870   48
4. The Ottoman Empire in 1870   50
5. The Austro-Hungrian Empire in 1870   54
6. The Russia Empire in 1870   61
7. The British Empire in 1870   82
8. The Italian States   87
9. The Western Front   129

Foreword

If the twentieth century is only a postscript to the nineteenth, the last quarter of the nineteenth century is the engine-room of the contemporary world. In those final decades, spilling over into the Great War, the great pillars of the democratic, industrial, capitalist world were constructed. In the forefront was the emergence of powerful nation states. Not only were the obvious nations, notably Germany and Italy, unified so too were Britain, France and, to a lesser extent, Spain. Where there had been a kaleidoscope of diverse regions, customs and cultures, by 1900 a single legal system, a national language and modern urban social structures and ways of life were coming to dominate. In other words, the world we still inhabit was being born. This was, of course, no simple process. Capitalism in its various forms including free market and state-sponsored variants brought terrible contradictions. Untold luxury for some; dire poverty and neglect for others. Urban living standards by and large rose but the globalisation of agricultural production, through transport and refrigeration revolutions, which brought cheap food from the Americas and the Antipodes, created a rural Great Depression in western Europe and sparked off peasant crises in Russia, the Balkans and eastern Europe in general. Capitalist complexity gave birth to fierce critics in the socialist and anarchist movements.

More modestly and at great cost to its pioneers, the trade union movement began to evolve into important working-class self-defence organisations. The emergence of mass societies and the mass media can be traced directly to the 1880s and 1890s. The spread of the franchise followed the shifts in social power. Only slowly, however, did the growth of wider voting do anything to dislodge the ruling class. By a series of clever adaptations the masses of new voters were largely harnessed to existing political parties and programmes, including, extraordinarily, the conservative movements of Europe whose fundamental existence had been based on opposing the rise of democracy and popular power. In many countries they eventually became its main beneficiaries. The country that most resisted political adaptation of this kind was Tsarist Russia and it is no coincidence that it was precisely here that radical revolutionary forces had their major success.

In this volume Robert Johnson focuses firmly on the central issues – nations; nationalism; chauvinism; the new imperialism and the complications which resulted in the Great War. In so doing he provides an excellent guide to the political foundations on which the late-nineteenth-century world, and therefore our world, was built. No student could fail to benefit from the information, concepts and well-thought out and stimulating exercises and discussion points presented by the author. History is a vitally important and serious subject but, in Robert Johnson's hands, learning is an active, enjoyable and satisfying process.

Chris Read, Professor of Modern European History, University of Warwick

Preface

This Studymate guide is designed to help you acquire an understanding of the key features of European history as rapidly as possible. As a student you will be faced with considerable pressure on your time, and with the need to read widely to obtain as many different historical opinions as you can, this guide will give you a secure knowledge of the fundamental parts of Europe's history between 1870 and 1918. Whether you are studying themes in European history, such as nationalism, socialism, democracy, liberalism, reaction or war, this Studymate will help you to acquire the relevant knowledge with minimum fuss. It will draw your attention to the details, examples and evidence. It will introduce you to arguments used by historians, and the points where controversies have arisen. It will help you to progress by means of study tips and helpful advice, as well as self-test units. The format has been designed to enable to you to tackle each topic in a series of small sections, each of which is easily digestible. There is no padding; it takes you straight to the heart of the issue.

The guide is by no means exhaustive, but it will enable you to acquire the critical information quickly. To assist you further, the guide also points to additional sources, reading and web sites. These will enhance your understanding, or provide you with more detail. This Studymate will take you through the key elements of the subject by means of the 'big questions', but without sacrificing specific detail and examples. The dates will reflect the important changes that occurred in Europe in this period. It will cover elements of the AS or A2 options (by AQA, Edexcel and OCR), but also the material covered by first and second year university core courses.

The format: questions, themes and historiography

This Studymate has been designed to tackle the key questions of this era in European history, and, as such, adopts a questioning approach throughout. Many of the questions posed reflect the most common questions students face in examinations or seminars. The guide is laid out in a chronological order, but is also designed to allow the reader to follow a thematic path through nation states, covering such concepts as nationalism, anti-Semitism, imperialism or socialism. It will also assist you in a search for continuities in European diplomacy including the question of European integration and disintegration which is at the core of current debates. Knowledge and use of concepts in students' work makes a considerable difference in grades achieved. Those who can grasp the overall themes of European history in this period (such as the development of capitalist economies, imperialism, international rivalries and the growth of the mass market, mass media, or popular politics), and write about them, will score highly. Most important of all, the guide contains information, in summary, of historians' views and where those views conflict. An understanding and appreciation of historians' opinions will enable you to acknowledge work which exists already in this field, and to challenge others' views, or obtain support for your own arguments. An ability to synthesise the debates which exist in history is the hallmark of a top candidate. You can find out more about improving your performance and developing your skills as an historian in *Studying History* (Studymate).

At the end of each chapter there are study tips, discussion topics and questions for you to tackle. Completion of these will enable you to check that you have understood the topic and that you really 'know' it.

This book is dedicated to the memory of the late Brian Elvins, an inspirational history teacher who was moderate, considerate and generous in equal measure.

Robert Johnson 2003

Europe in 1870: Nation States, the Capitalist Economy and Society

One-minute summary – In this first chapter, the character of Europe in 1870 is explained. In essence, Europe was undergoing a transformation because of industrialisation, urbanisation and a rapid population growth. Accompanying these shifts were social changes of deep significance: old rural structures of deference and loyalty to the rich were being eroded or replaced by new individualist aspirations. Amongst the élites there were doubts about the future and ever more radical, or reactionary, solutions were proposed. New ideas were gaining wide-spread support, thanks to the development of mass media, and new transport and communication networks. Europe was gradually polarizing ideologically between the democratic and 'left wing' tendency for reform and representation, and the 'right wing' tendency to impose controls. Paradoxically, the concept of nationalism served as a social cement in this time of division. It was an idea favoured by both the left and the right. The left saw nationalism as the will of the masses who shared a common identity and pursued a common purpose. The right saw nationalism as a concept that put the duty to the fatherland as a higher purpose than the interests of the individual or the class to which they belonged. This meant that nationalist feelings could supersede any class conflict and make the masses loyal to the state. However, the European states were embroiled in a deep rivalry with each other, a situation that manifested itself in war or imperialist competition.

In this chapter you will learn:

▶ the status of the European states
▶ how the European economies were transformed by industrialisation
▶ how the social classes in Europe were organised
▶ the diplomatic situation in 1870.

The European states

The European states were divided into Great Powers and minor powers

In 1870, the group of European states with the greatest wealth and military power were Great Britain, France, Prussia, the Austro-Hungarian Empire and Russia. On the periphery of Europe, the Ottoman Empire continued its steady decline through corruption and mismanagement, a process that had begun as early as the seventeenth century. The other states of Europe were, by contrast, small in territorial extent and less powerful. There was no united Germany, this region being merely a 'geographical expression', Italy was not yet complete and the

Balkans were still dominated by the Turks who had acquired the area in the 1500s. There were some disparities of wealth between the western states of Europe and the provinces of the east, in that the western powers were based on maritime trade and a rapid industrialisation, and their political systems generally favoured greater liberalism and enterprise. In the east, the economies were still agrarian and the systems of rule were more authoritarian and less dynamic.

Great Britain was often the envy of other Europeans

Britain had been the first of the European states to make the transition to an industrialised economy, and by 1870 it had one of the most urbanised populations in Europe. Its wealth was considerable and its manufacturing base made it the hub in a circulation of global trade. In addition, it had been the first to create financial services and so was the world's most important banker and insurance broker. It had a vast merchant fleet, protected by a great navy, and was on the way to becoming the world's largest colonial empire. The vibrancy and importance of Britain is reflected in the title of the epoch: the Victorian Age. Britain was also a parliamentary democracy with a limited franchise based on property ownership, and ruled by a constitutional monarch (a ruler restricted in power by a democratically elected assembly called Parliament). The upper chamber of this Parliament was called the House of Lords, and, until 1911, was the most powerful body. Its members were not elected but were appointed by the monarch or received their status through hereditary rights. The lower chamber, or House of Commons, was elected every seven years and was dominated by two political parties, the Conservatives and the Liberals. The majority party formed the government, the decisions being made by a select group called the Cabinet led by a Prime Minister. A separate judiciary meant that the British political system consisted of a series of checks and balances, each element of government being denied absolute power. It was an attractive model for others in Europe.

The Emperor in France was becoming unpopular

From the 1850s, France was ruled by the Emperor Napoleon III, nephew of the great Napoleon Bonaparte. Napoleon III had seized power through a *coup d'état*, and ruled as a dictator, but he had restored some political freedoms in the years that followed. However, his aggressive or inconsistent foreign policy had alienated other powers in Europe and France had no allies by 1870. In addition, at home, there was growing opposition to the lack of real democracy. France gave the appearance of a being a liberal system but it was not. The ministers he appointed were selected for personal loyalty rather than ability. The *Conseil d'état* was a bureaucracy that served only the Emperor. The Senate was an upper chamber whose members were appointed for life by the Emperor, and the *Corps Legislatif*, the lower house, was denied the right to introduce or amend legislation, even though it was elected by universal manhood suffrage every six years. France had enjoyed a period of unprecedented prosperity but the so-called Third Party, which opposed the government, managed to force some concessions from Napoleon. The legislature and the Senate gained more power (they could propose laws, criticise and vote against the budget and nominate officials). In a plebiscite in May 1870, Napoleon's liberal measures were approved by the majority of Frenchmen, but a significant number voted against him, especially those in the big cities of Paris, Lyon and Marseilles.

Prussia was an autocratic and aggressive state

Prussia was ruled by King Wilhelm I of the Hohenzollern dynasty. His chief minister was Otto von Bismarck, a former ambassador to Russia and a member of the aristocratic élite. Prussia had been enlarged at the end of the Napoleonic Wars and was the biggest of all the German states. However, the patchwork of little dukedoms and provinces all looked to Austria for protection and leadership. Sensing that, in the future, Prussia would face either the humiliation of remaining under the Austrian Empire's influence in central Europe or the prospect of being subsumed into a united, liberal-dominated Germany, Bismarck looked for ways of increasing Prussia's power. Bismarck later claimed that he had planned the unification of Germany under Prussian leadership from the start, but, in fact, he appeared to steer Prussia through a series of separate diplomatic and military situations that ended with a united Germany. In 1866, he persuaded the north German states to join Prussia in a successful war against Austria and this left Prussia as the leading power of the whole confederation. Bismarck was also eager to prevent the growth of democratic and liberal movements in Prussia and in Germany. Mindful of revolutionary unrest that had occurred in 1848 (when the monarchy temporarily lost control of the country), he had been appointed to defeat the liberals in the Prussian assembly and save the monarchy. He restricted the press and ignored the liberal parliamentary protests, using a sense of nationalism to overcome opposition.

Austria-Hungary faced internal difficulties

The Austro-Hungarian Empire was a multi-racial state dominated by the Austrians and ruled by the Emperor Franz-Josef. Until 1866, the Empire had dominated central Europe and the Habsburg monarchy had a pedigree of rule that stretched back to the 1500s. Within the Empire, the monarchy was an institution that commanded almost medieval loyalty from its subject peoples, and was probably the key factor that held the state together. The Roman Catholic Church also provided a unifying bond given the proximity of the Muslim Ottoman Empire which had been an enemy for hundreds of years. The population of 30 million were divided by language, culture and nationality. There were Poles, Czechs, Slovaks, Italians, Ruthenes, Romanians, Germans, Serbs, Slovenes, Croats, and, most important of all, Austrians and Magyars (the people of Hungary). In 1866, Austria had been defeated by the Prussians and the Magyars used the opportunity to assert their own interests in a movement called the *Ausgleich*. As a result, the Empire was known as the Dual Monarchy, the Emperor of Austria being acknowledged now only as the King of Hungary. The government met alternately at the capitals of Austria and Hungary, Vienna and Budapest, but each state had its own parliament and government. Nevertheless, the national aspirations of the other races were ignored and suppressed.

Russia was an autocratic state undergoing great changes

Russia was the largest of all the European states, and was, in fact, also the most powerful Asian power. Its sprawling possessions and many races were ruled by the Tsar, an autocrat with unlimited powers justified by divine appointment (an idea long discredited in the West). In the 1860s, Tsar Alexander II had embarked on a programme of apparently liberal reform in an attempt to catch up with the rest of Europe. He was aware that since the Napoleonic Wars, Russia had fallen behind in industrial development. Russia had even been defeated on its own soil in the Crimean War (1854–56) by Britain, France, Turkey and Piedmont. Alexander proceeded with change cautiously, hoping to avoid the worst consequences of industrialisation and political agitation that he observed in the West. Serfdom was abolished in 1861, but both peasants and landowners were still restricted by debts which prevented the modernisation of agriculture. Most Russians lived in abject poverty under the rule of the privileged few. Local government reforms were also stillborn, and Alexander grew impatient with the growth of opposition groups. He returned to a policy of repression when terrorist organisations tried to assassinate him. To secure Russia and improve its economic potential, Alexander's foreign policy continued in a traditional vein: territorial expansion southwards into the Balkans and the shrinking Ottoman territories, or into Central Asia and the Far East.

Italy was united but its people were divided

Italy was unified in 1860 by the revolutionary leader Garibaldi and the Prime Minister of Piedmont, Camillo de Cavour. However, as a recently united state, it lacked the strength to be considered a Great Power. Although Cavour favoured industrial progress and liberal politics, he ensured that Piedmont was the leading province within the new Italy by ruthless centralisation. The Piedmontese king, Victor Emmanuel II was a constitutional monarch for all of Italy, but the disappointment of southern Italians at the lack of improvement after unification made him an unpopular figure. When Cavour died in 1861, no one seemed able to develop a greater sense of unity in the country and regional loyalties remained strong. Lombardy and Venetia were acquired from Austria in 1866 (because of the Prussian victory) even though Italian forces had been defeated, and Rome became the capital when the French garrison of the city left in 1870. Despite these achievements, northern Italian troops were ordered to occupy the south to prevent civil war; such was the depth of anger and resentment there. Corruption, political instability, poverty and a lack of industrial resources stunted the development of Italy for decades.

European economies and industrialisation

Economic changes had a profound impact on European history

The economic history of Europe from 1870 is closely tied to the processes of industrialisation, urbanisation and population growth. Rural migration to the cities and new technologies in production combined and accelerated from the mid-nineteenth century. Increasingly, as cheaper goods were produced, trade was stimulated and new wealth accumulated. The cities and their factories acted as vortices for the poorer of society, many of whom were being driven from the land by hardship, population growth, or the attractions of the regular labour and wages of industry. The shift from a largely agrarian system to a modern, industrial base caused, in turn, a profound shift in politics, military power, social relations and ideas. The existing rivalry of the European powers was sharpened by the speed of industrialisation, some powers surging ahead while others lagged behind. It has been suggested that the countries could be divided into the 'first' and 'second' industrialised nations, a dynamic that altered the balance of power on the continent. The spread of nationalism combined with the development of new military power, a process greatly influenced by the advance in technology and industrial techniques (see Robert Johnson, *The Changing Nature of Warfare*, Studymates, 2002), leading to an impulse of global imperialism. In this rarefied atmosphere of competition and rivalry, and a not inconsiderable fear of the future, it is easier to understand why the European powers plunged into war in 1914.

The powers were unbalanced

The populations of the European states give a first indication of the manpower potential they could muster. The levels of production in the staple industries of iron and steel also indicate the relative strength of each power, and a clue to their military potential, but per capita levels of industrialisation give the clearest differences between the European states.

Total populations of the leading world powers, 1890–1913 (millions)

	1890	1900	1913
Russia	116.8	135.6	175.1
United States	62.6	75.9	97.3
Germany	49.2	56.0	66.9
Austria-Hungary	42.6	46.7	52.1
Japan	39.9	43.8	51.3
France	38.3	38.9	39.7
Great Britain	37.4	41.1	45.6
Italy	30.0	32.2	35.1

Iron and steel production of the world's leading powers, 1890–1913 (millions of tons) iron shown in 1890, steel for 1900 and 1910.

	1890	1900	1913
United States	9.3	10.3	31.8
Great Britain	8.0	5.0	7.7
Germany	4.1	6.3	17.6
France	1.9	1.5	4.6
Austria-Hungary	0.9	1.1	2.6
Russia	0.9	2.2	4.8
Japan	0.02	N/a	0.2
Italy	0.01	0.1	0.9

Per capita levels of industrialisation, 1880–1913 (compared with Great Britain in 1900 = 100)

	1880	1900	1913
Great Britain	87	**100**	115
United States	38	69	126
France	28	39	59
Germany	25	52	85
Italy	12	17	26
Austria-Hungary	15	23	32
Russia	10	15	20
Japan	9	12	20

Economic activity was changing

In 1870, much of the economic activity of Europe was still agricultural. Peasant workers conducted farming on small acreages, their small incomes being subsidised by their own food supply. They had no economic protection against failed harvests, accident or illness. Yet the mass majority of these peasant farmers did not own their own land, renting it from landowners who were drawn from the aristocratic nobility. Falling land values meant that these landowners faced a bleak future of loss of income and indebtedness. By contrast, the industrial activity of Europe was undergoing a rapid expansion. As extractive and manufacturing industries were initially very labour intensive, large workforces were required and these, with their families, created a spectacular growth in urbanisation, further stimulating the construction industry and food retailing. City life was nevertheless divided sharply between the bad quality residential and working areas of the workforces, and the genteel wards of the rich. Those who owned the industries, or supported them through a range of clerical, legal and financial services benefited hugely from industrialisation. They developed a taste for the privileges normally reserved for the aristocratic élite, from *haute cuisine* to political power.

The prevailing economic ideas of free trade and protection

The increase of industrialisation, with the mass production of goods to a uniform standard, led to a corresponding burgeoning of trading activity. The exchange of products across oceans and international boundaries without uniform systems of currency or measurements entailed risks, and insurance or other financial services emerged to protect traders and manufacturers. Britain's early lead in this development quickly made London the world's financial services capital. Its overwhelming capacity in the mid-nineteenth century threatened to swamp other embryonic manufacturing industries and their national governments opted for protective tariffs (taxes on foreign imports). By contrast, the British, who could produce goods more cheaply and abundantly than ever before, urged other countries to adopt a 'free trade' policy. The thinking was that a free exchange of goods would assist manufacturers, but also the consumer (who would pay less for the imports), and this, in turn, would stimulate more demand and growth. Ultimately, it was thought, all the European states would be trading freely with each other. This level of mutual co-operation, it was hoped, would ensure more peaceful relations between the nations. In the 1860s, Britain was able to persuade, and sometimes force, other countries to change to a free trade arrangement, but there were already signs by 1870 that the European powers wished to protect their own manufacturers (and big farmers) from the fierce blast of competition from Britain, and also from the United States.

Social classes in Europe

The élites dominated European affairs

Europe in 1870 was still dominated in political, financial, social and property terms by a very small élite. In Great Britain there were some 5,500 families who owned most of the land and this form of wealth was still seen as the hallmark of power and prestige. David Cannadine has calculated that the British aristocracy was the richest and proportionally the greatest land-owning élite of Europe. In Russia, although the nobility owned a massive 177 million acres, this made up only 14 per cent of the available land. In France, less than 20 per cent of the land was owned by the old élite. In Prussia, the aristocratic *Junkers* owned 40 per cent of the land, but most of the estates were below 1,000 acres. Similarly in Spain, although 52 per cent was held by the old nobility, the estates were small. Of the greatest landowners, only a handful of families in Eastern Europe possessed the scale of holdings of their British counterparts.

The élites' status was changing but they retained considerable power

In addition, the very status of the landed élites was less valued in Europe than in the British Isles. When monarchy was abolished in France, the titles of the nobility went with them. In Prussia and Russia, indebtedness, the break-up of the estates to pay off these burdens and a proliferation of new ennoblements weakened the prestige of the old élites. In Austria there were 9,000 new ennoblements between 1800 and 1914, creating an élite of 250,000. There were 600,000 hereditary nobles in Russia, and the corrupt misuse of titles in Italy meant there were 12,000 aristocrats there by 1906. Yet, despite these weaknesses, the aristocrats of Europe remained close to the seat of power in each case. They provided the ministers, generals and chief advisors to the crowned heads of the continent. Inevitably, they often served their own interests, although these often coincided with the interests of their nation state. Many of them felt a strong sense of feudal duty towards both the rulers and the poor, but they expected privileges from the monarchs and obedience from the masses in return. The monarchs themselves faced demands for limits to their powers. These were successfully imposed in Britain, Italy and France, but Prussia, Austria-Hungary and Russia remained autocratic. Autocratic monarchs operated above the law and were still deeply involved in all national decision-making.

The middle classes were growing rapidly

Industrialisation, and the growth of manufacturing and a service sector, led to an explosion of so-called 'white collar' employment. These middle classes, or *bourgeoisie*, acquired a considerable share of the new wealth and they developed a corresponding desire to gain political influence. They grew in numbers in the national assemblies of Europe, and were ever more critical of the rulers that denied them real power. Their value system also began to make itself felt. Although some aspired to the life of the aristocracy and a country estate, they were generally more urbane, modern in taste and progressive in politics. There were limits and exceptions to this broad generalisation and it is misleading to speak of a middle class as if it were some homogenous group. The *bourgeoisie* embraced a diverse range of professions and incomes, from a rural clerk to the super-rich magnate of mining operations. In the states of Eastern Europe, they were small in number compared with the West. They were champions of their own national identities, and competitive within their own class. Despite their social mobility, they maintained a strict hierarchy of status in their own clubs and salons. Although they favoured progressive politics against the nobility, they often bitterly opposed the same aspirations in the lower classes and tended to favour the stern maintenance of law and order above radicalism and agitation. However, as a result of their growth in numbers and influence, the period is sometimes dubbed 'the *bourgeois* century'.

The urban working classes lived and worked in tough conditions

By 1870, a new generation had grown up that knew only the urban life of industrial work. The ties and traditions of rural life began to fall away, as the industrial labour force grew accustomed to the regulation and discipline of the workplace. In the factory the timings and routine of the day were strictly enforced, a situation reinforced by the production line. The sheer momentum of the machinery imposed a new pace of life on the worker, and his time and labour were exchanged for wages. Hoping to maximise profits by keeping overhead costs to a minimum, industrialists tried to suppress these wages. In the face of this exploitation, and confronted with harsh working conditions (namely long hours and dangerous practices), workers began to organise themselves and refuse to work unless their terms were met. In some cases, this provoked a severe reaction from the state or from their employers. Those in the poorest situations could hardly afford to go on strike lest they lose their jobs altogether.

Workers were regarded as a revolutionary force
In this environment of bitter labour relations, more radical political solutions were discussed. New ideas of socialism and revolution were considered. Yet, in the most advanced industrial states of the West (which were also the most liberal), concessions were more readily granted. Where the numbers of urban workers were small, as in the East, the élites were less willing to make concessions and were eager to act against them. The urban workers, once referred to as the proletariat, were a diverse group, made up a plethora of professions and trades. They were often loyal to their nation state rather than to any idea of a 'class'. Whilst they were prepared to act aggressively in defence of their own interests, the most remarkable feature of the period is how much punishment they endured without serious revolutionary action. They possessed a quiet pride in their background, enforced a hierarchy within their local communities (and between genders) and appeared to be more deferential than revolutionary agitators would have liked, and subsequently more than historians would wish to acknowledge.

The rural populations and the urban poor faced a lifetime of hardship
The poor were the majority of European society in 1870. Many were at risk of starvation, even in the great cities, and malnutrition, or diseases associated with it, was common. They lacked any education, relying often on the consolations of Christianity for their guidance. Medical care was patchy, and traditional remedies were still the norm. In the face of greater industrialisation, urbanisation and the demands of their social superiors, the poor clung to their traditional rights as long as possible and invoked their religious doctrines as justification. Denied a share of the wealth that industrial life generated, many chose to rebel. There were old artisan Luddites who smashed machines, rioters who took on the forces of order, but there were millions more who rejected the middle-class values of toleration and moderation and used alcohol as the only escape from a harsh world. Demoralisation was common, and manifested itself in crime, prostitution, suicide, mental illness and domestic violence. The poor were as divided, stratified

and territorial as the other classes, despite a strong sense of community amongst certain groups. The street in urban areas, or the village in the countryside, was the focus of their loyalty, although regional and national loyalty could be expressed just as exuberantly. Extended families supported each other, and neighbourliness was essential for survival, being the conduit of moral support, provision of a crèche or information on the availability of casual jobs. Those who got work found that it was unskilled, tough and low paid. Employment might still come through the hiring fairs (being picked out by an employer for a day's work), but with no welfare system, old age, illness or disability might condemn poor people to a workhouse (in Britain), prison, or death.

The prevailing social and political ideas were of liberalism and conservativism

The middle classes often favoured the extension of political power to their social groups, whilst protecting property and preventing too many state restrictions on industry. They favoured keeping taxation to a minimum and wanted to avoid state intervention in the lives and lifestyles of their class, a notion called *laissez faire*. Collectively, this concept was known as liberalism, and, in its more radical form, it seemed to offer the chance for the gradual development of political rights to the lower classes at some point in the future. The opposite of this concept was conservativism. This idea was favoured by the élites, who saw only anarchy and ruin for both nation state and themselves, if power was transferred to the masses. They aimed to conserve and protect their property and privileges through their existing hold on power. These concepts were used by groups with certain interests, but two more universal ideas also developed in this period.

Universal ideas offered unity

Socialism advocated full state ownership of all property and the abolition of capitalism. It called on all those of the working classes and poor to unite against an exploitative system. In its moderate form, it was thought this could be achieved through a peaceful and gradual process, particularly through reforms passed by the government. Radicals favoured direct action, namely a revolution to overthrow the élites by force. Exacting a terrible revenge for their oppression, the élites would be compelled to give up their property or be killed. Yet, the concept of nationalism seemed to offer a chance to avoid the terrible consequences of revolution and civil conflict. Favoured by most classes, nationalism excluded only outsiders and embraced social unity. The common bonds of language, culture, religion or territory were attractive because they offered a strong sense of identity and place in a period of bewildering change. National pride could be adopted by the individual, promoting even the poorest of society to a feeling that he or she was better than the foreigner. In both socialist and nationalist circles, symbolism, songs and literature were produced, but the concept of socialism remained bedded in the radical traditions of agitators, whilst nationalism was fostered by the existing élites as a means of preserving the *status quo*.

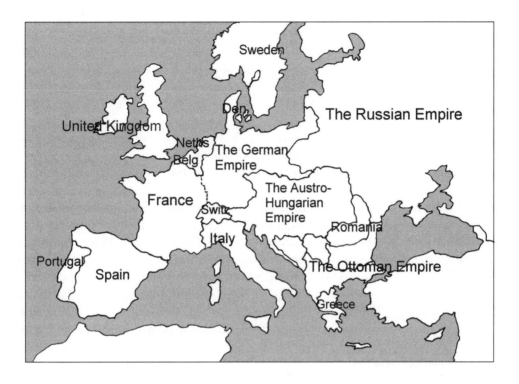

Figure 1. Europe in 1870.

The diplomatic situation in 1870

Sources of conflict: the Balkans

There were a number of potential flashpoints in Europe, but few were more significant than the Balkans. The decay of the Ottoman Empire had already resulted in a clash between the Great Powers in the Crimean War, but it was the nationalist revolt of the Greeks in the 1820s that represented the first great rent in the rotting fabric of Turkish rule. The Egyptians had defeated the Turks in the 1830s. Romania became independent in 1858, and Christians in the provinces of Bulgaria, Serbia and Montenegro were growing restless against their Muslim overlords. The Turks were, in fact, reliant on Britain and France to maintain their territorial integrity at all. These powers believed the threat of Russian annexation of the Balkans outweighed the desire for national liberation in the region. If Russia were to defeat Turkey and control the Straits near Constantinople, it was feared the Tsarist empire would dominate the Eastern Mediterranean menacing British rule in India, trade arteries through the region and French influence in the Near East. Austria-Hungary also feared that Russian control of the Balkans would weaken her position and give Russia a strategically valuable 'second front' on her southern borders. Containing Russia became a key aspect of Austro-Hungarian foreign policy.

Franco-German rivalry was acute

In 1870, Prussia and the German states stood on the brink of war with France. Prussia's efforts to unite Germany under its leadership could only be thwarted by France, which did not wish to see a powerful rival on its eastern border. France was diplomatically isolated, Napoleon III's inconsistent, aggressive and grasping foreign policy having alienated all the other states of Europe. The rivalry between the Germans and the French was to remain a source of conflict for decades.

Anglo-Russian rivalry: Central Asia, Afghanistan and the Far East

Great Britain already possessed an extensive maritime empire by 1870, but the 'Jewel in the Crown' of its colonial territories was India. Russian expansion into Central Asia appeared to threaten the landward and mountainous borders of India. Britain had temporarily occupied Afghanistan in 1838–42 as a buffer zone, but settled on the Punjab as a suitable border from the late 1840s. Similarly, Russian expansion into the Far East, such as the Amur Province, and a preference for ruthless economic protectionism, seemed to threaten British commercial hegemony in the moribund China. Britain and Russia were thus rivals for influence in Asia. This was only the start of an imperial rivalry that would soon overtake all the European powers, and subjugate the peoples of Africa and Asia.

International co-operation

It would be misleading to suggest that Europeans saw each other only as rivals. The Napoleonic Wars had shown that faced with the prospect of one power dominating the whole continent, others would act together to prevent it. Moreover, improving communications technology (such as the telegraph and railways) could prevent the prospect of diplomatic misunderstandings. The establishment of the Red Cross in 1863 by Henri Dunant, also indicated that respect for international bodies could be of considerable benefit to Europe. The postal service was organised across the continent in 1875, as was recognition of International Copyright, and then came the far more significant International Court of The Hague in 1899. The first legal regulations of war were soon established, banning the use of poison gas, exploding bullets and incendiary projectiles. In 1907, the International Office of Public Health was established. Cars, telephones, and aircraft all speeded up communications and offered a hope of greater integration.

The Great War was a tragedy for Europe

However, in the end, all these technologies and developments were to no avail in preserving peace. In fact, these same technologies were soon harnessed for war. Even the agreed restrictions of the Hague Convention were overturned in the Great War of 1914–18. This conflict, the result of years of rivalry and international tension, was a disaster for Europe. Millions perished, millions more were maimed, régimes were overthrown, and empires collapsed. The world's first genocide of the twentieth century was perpetrated against the Christian

Armenians by the Muslim Turks in 1915. Extreme political ideas were born, and, after the war, against a background of further economic hardship, these ideas swept thousands into the arms of ruthless dictators like Lenin, Mussolini, Stalin, and Hitler.

Tutorial

Progress questions

1. Account for Great Britain's leading position in Europe between 1870 and 1914.

2. What factors seemed to drive European rivalry in the period before 1900?

3. What impact did industrialisation have on the Europeans in general?

4. Why can this period be considered a '*bourgeois*' era?

Discussion points

1. How far was European rivalry based on levels of economic development?

2. 'The late nineteenth century was significant not because it was a period of struggle between the *nations*, but between the *ancien régimes* (old orders) and the new aspirant classes of the industrial revolution.' Do you agree with this assessment of the period 1870–1913?

Practical assignment

1. Taking a map of the European continent, try to create a sketch map of the territorial extent of each of the nations, and annotate onto the edge of the map notes about each country taken from this chapter.

2. Using the figures from the tables in this chapter, create a histogram of levels of development. Add an evaluation to your charts, suggesting a rank order for the powers.

Study and revision tips

1. This chapter gives an outline of the condition of Europe in 1870. Try to get a feel for the relative strengths of the countries and the issues that confronted them internally, but do not worry if, at this stage, the material appears to be complex. It will become clearer as you browse through the next few chapters.

2. You may find it useful to make a few brief notes of your own, or use a highlighter pen, to pick out the key information from this chapter about the leading powers and their rulers, or the systems of government.

3. Notice what political ideas were being used in this period. If you do not yet feel confident with these, try to create a glossary list with an explanation of each one.

2

France: From Second Empire to The Third Republic

One-minute summary – The unpopular Second Empire of Napoleon III was destroyed by the Franco-Prussian War of 1870–71, but the Third Republic that replaced it was plagued by internal division and remained militarily weak. France was also diplomatically isolated until the 1890s. However, despite a series of crises, such as the Dreyfus Case and the Panama Scandal, the Republic survived, even enduring the trial of the First World War. This fact, and its surprising collapse in 1940, has prompted historians to speculate on the actual and apparent strength of the Third Republic.

In this chapter you will learn:

▶ how the Second Empire came to an end
▶ the significance of the Franco-Prussian War, 1870–71
▶ how the Republic dealt with internal threats to its stability
▶ the nature of the foreign policy of the Republic
▶ historical controversies about the period.

The Second Empire

Napoleon III was challenged by calls for greater democracy

The Emperor Napoleon III faced growing domestic opposition to the lack of real democracy in the late 1860s. When a cousin of the Emperor shot a well-known republican journalist, Victor Noir, in January 1870, the funeral became the focus of a demonstration against Napoleon. The so-called Third Party, which opposed the government, had managed to force some concessions from Napoleon by uniting with 40 left-wing deputies. The legislature had gained more power (they could propose laws, criticise and vote against the budget and nominate officials) and Emille Oliver led the opposition to the restrictions of the emperor. In April 1870, the Senate was also granted the right to legislate. To alter the constitution like this, the Bonapartist party called a plebiscite on Napoleon's reforms in May 1870. The majority of Frenchmen (7.5 million) approved Napoleon's liberal measures, but a significant number (1.5 million) voted against him, especially in the big cities of Paris, Lyon and Marseilles. Napoleon was largely dependent on his bureaucracy and selected ministers to rule, and he sought popular policies that could bolster his position.

The Franco-Prussian War, 1870–71

War was a result of the *realpolitik* (power politics) ambitions of France and Prussia
Having alienated Austria in the 1860s by inconsistency in his foreign policy, Napoleon found himself isolated in Europe. Great Britain had grown wary of him because of his designs on Luxembourg and the Low Countries (strategically close to the British coast), the Russian Tsar believed he was an adventurer masquerading as an emperor, and Bismarck saw France as an obstacle to Prussian expansion in the German Confederation. Napoleon tried to oppose the Prussian candidature to a vacancy for the Spanish throne, but Bismarck cleverly altered a conciliatory diplomatic retort from the Prussian King Wilhelm I while he was on holiday at Ems. The infamous Ems telegram was greeted with outrage in France, but the Cabinet had already decided on war unless the Prussians made a total withdrawal of any claim to the Spanish crown (France feared the Prussians would install a pro-German puppet regime on the southern border). The real cause of the war lay deeper than the telegram. Bismarck knew that Napoleon was a threat (as the Emperor had already demanded compensation), and a war would finally persuade Austria it could have no alliance with France, thus reducing its influence over Germany for good. The Empress, Eugenie, the minister Gramont, and the French military command all believed that war would benefit France because it would keep the German states divided and reunite the French people. Leboeuf, the War Minister, had told the Cabinet that the French army was ready 'down to the last gaiter button'. War was declared on 19 July 1870.

The war was one of great significance
Although the French went on to the attack in the Saar, they were soon thrown back at Worth and Spicheren on 6 August. Marshal Bezaine was besieged at Metz, and Napoleon joined the Army of Châlons. Realising that to fall back on the defences of Paris would be politically unpopular, Napoleon and Marshal MacMahon tried to outflank the German forces in a move that would eventually relieve Metz. In fact, the Germans encircled MacMahon's army at Sedan and it was forced to surrender on 2 September and 84,000 men were captured. On 4 September, rioting in Paris prompted the Assembly (parliament) to depose Napoleon and proclaim a republic. Although the new government tried to fight on, Jules Favre, the new Minister of the Interior, tried to negotiate an end to the war on 18 September. These talks failed and Paris was besieged. Leon Gambetta, a republican leader, escaped the siege in a hot air balloon to organise resistance in the provinces. However, Bezaine surrendered Metz on 27 October, and the provincial forces were all defeated: Generals Chanzy at Le Mans, Faidherbe at Saint Quentin and Bourbaki at Belfort. Paris surrendered on 28 January 1871. The leading military power of Europe had been defeated and the balance of power had shifted decisively to Prussia and its German allies.

The Republic: internal threats to stability

The Third Republic began with a civil war

The Germans insisted that, before peace could be agreed, the French must present one representative delegation. Accordingly, elections were held across France on 8 February 1871. Whilst the republicans wanted to continue the war (*'la guerre a outrance'*), the monarchists did not, and they had the majority of the French people behind them. Few Frenchmen could see any benefit in a war with no prospect of victory. The new National Assembly (13 February 1871) had 400 monarchist deputies, but only 200 republicans. The ministry of Adolphe Thiers was formed and had to accept the harsh German peace terms. The Treaty of Frankfurt (May) stated that France lost Alsace and Lorraine, she had to pay five milliards of Francs as a war indemnity and had to accept an army of occupation for three years, the period over which the payment was to be made. However, anger at the acceptance of defeat prompted several provincial risings. Fear of a royalist restoration (especially as the new assembly had met at Versailles – the old royal seat of government), and the disarming of the Paris National Guard by troops from the provinces of France, as well as an edict from Thiers' government that all back rents and debts had to be paid to their landlords, sparked a full-scale rebellion known as the Commune in Paris on 19 April. The Communards rejected Thiers's government, and, although politically divided, hoped that a series of local governments would emerge, each with its own budget and military force. Thiers believed that the Commune had to be suppressed to prevent anarchy and the total collapse of France. Street fighting lasted until 28 May, many of the rebels being summarily shot.

The way that the Republic had emerged left long-term problems

The other European powers regarded Republican France with suspicion. The First Republic of the French Revolution, 1791–1804, had been an aggressive state that plunged Europe into war. The Second Republic had been less successful, but had a reputation for revolutionary and extremist politics. However, the defeat of France made it appear that she was now a weak nation, so its future policy was uncertain. The crushing of the Commune also alienated many left wingers for decades. In the 1880s, the workers were suspicious of the régime that had been so eager to crush what they regarded later as a workers' revolt. This tended to push them towards more radical political ideas and away from the *bourgeois* politicians. However, the defeat, death or exile of the radicals in 1871, meant that many monarchists could accept the Republic as a moderate régime. For example, the Republicans suppressed radical demands for the abolition of private property. Thiers was also a middle-class moderate, and he rejected the extremism of the Commune, but other revolutionaries across Europe looked to the Commune as a symbol of resistance to bourgeois domination. In fact, the Commune was more about the age-old struggle between the independent Parisians and the centralising national government. The extreme conditions of the war and the hardships of the siege had brought matters to a head, although Paris kept its reputation for radical politics.

France quickly recovered but internal weaknesses continued

Despite the loss of the provinces of Alsace-Lorraine, France recovered quickly from the war. A programme of national reconstruction restored property and railways affected by the conflict. There was a popular desire to rid France of the German army of occupation, and, by September 1873, the war indemnity had been paid off. In 1872, the French army was also reorganised along Prussian lines, introducing a five-year term of service with several years on the reserve list. Yet, France remained internally divided.

The divisions between monarchists and republicans were clear cut

Monarchists had won the election of 1871 on the issue of ending the war quickly. However, although the royalists had a majority in the assembly, it was unclear if the French people would accept another monarch. To make matters worse, the royalists were split between Legitimist Bourbons (100 in the assembly), Orleanists (300) and Bonapartists (30). When the Bourbons put forward the Comte de Chambord as a candidate for the throne, the other royalists initially disagreed but hoped to reach some sort of compromise before the National Assembly was dissolved and new elections held. In 1873, it was agreed that, after the reign of the Comte de Chambord, the Comte de Paris (an Orleanist) would take over. Growing tired of the republican Thiers, the royalists replaced him with Marshal MacMahon, a monarchist Chief Executive. However, when the Comte de Chambord insisted on the restoration of the old symbols of the Bourbons, such as the Fleur de Lys flag, he was abandoned as a viable candidate. By 1875, Leon Gambetta and other Republicans had managed to persuade many Frenchmen that it was simply too difficult to find a compromise ruler. The Republicans gained a small majority in the Chamber of Deputies, and helped pass the Organic Laws, a provisional constitution that would fit either a limited monarchy or a Republic and be based on universal suffrage. By a majority of only one vote, the head of state was entitled the President of the Republic, and the Third Republic had been born.

The consolidation of Republican rule was achieved by MacMahon

The question of the President's powers was not addressed until 16 May 1877, when MacMahon compelled the Premier, the moderate Republican Jules Simon, to resign. MacMahon objected to Simon's half-hearted opposition to the left in the Chamber of Deputies. However, in protest, the Chamber of Deputies refused to approve the President's choice of Premier, the Orleanist duc de Broglie. Acting with the support of the Senate, the President dissolved the Chamber and called a new election. However, it was a short-lived triumph, for MacMahon was forced to accept a ministry put forward by the Chamber in December of that year. In 1879, the Republicans gained a majority in the senate as well as the Chamber of Deputies. MacMahon resigned and was replaced by Jules Grevy.

The Republicans passed a series of reforms to strengthen their influence

To win over the middle and lower classes, the exiled Communards were allowed to return (1880), freedom of assembly and freedom of the press was guaranteed (1881), trade unions were legalised (1884) and all municipal councils, except Paris, were allowed to elect their own mayors (1883). In addition, entry to the civil service was to be by competitive examination and not through patronage (1884). However, the most far reaching measures concerned the church. The Republicans aimed to limit the influence of the Catholic Church and to destroy its pro-monarchist political power. The Jesuits and other teaching orders were expelled. Teachers in religious schools had to take state examinations. In 1882, all primary education was placed in state hands, being free and compulsory for children aged 6 to 13. Charities and hospitals were also taken over by the state. Civil marriages and divorces were introduced. Finally, in 1884, the Republicans passed laws to prevent any form of revision of Republican government and to block any royal candidate from the presidency.

Opposition to the Republic came from the right and left wing

The right wing in France broadly encompassed the monarchists, the Catholic Church and the nobility, all of whom had lost their status to the Republicans. Nationalists in France allied with these right-wing groups, and the humiliation of the continued occupation of Alsace Lorraine generated widespread support for the nationalist cause. Amongst the most outspoken of the nationalists was Paul Deroulede and his League of Patriots, who called for a war of *revanche* (revenge) against Germany. On the left, radical socialists harboured a resentment of the Republican leaders because they believed they represented only bourgeois interests. The left wing wanted the Republican government to tackle working and living conditions. By the 1880s, the spread of Marxist and revolutionary ideas meant that, in theory at least, the left could pose a threat to the stability of the republic.

The Boulanger Affair threatened the Republic

The first great threat to the survival of the Republic occurred between 1886 and 1889 during the so-called Boulanger Affair. In the 1880s, the monarchists had lost their hopes for a royal restoration. The Prince Imperial (Bonaparte's son) was killed in Zululand in 1879, and the Comte de Chambord died in 1883. As a result, the royalists looked for a strong national leader who could replace the Republic or restore their privileges. Many workers were also distressed by the economic depression of the 1880s and were looking for an alternative to the bourgeois governments of the republic. In 1885, the right did well in the elections in France. General Georges Boulanger was made Minister of War following a successful career as military governor of Tunis (occupied in 1881). He made a series of speeches condemning the government, and calling for a war of revenge to recover Alsace-Lorraine. He advocated improvements to the living conditions of soldiers. His celebrity status and his ability to weld together supporters on the left and right made him a popular figure. When the government fell, he lost his office, but he applied for a place in the Chamber of Deputies even though he was not eligible. Even when the government declared him retired from the 'active list' of the army, he was elected to the Chamber. In 1889, the government decided this popular man was a danger to the Republic and ordered his arrest. Boulanger, who could have summoned the support of millions, lost his nerve and fled to Brussels. Humiliated, he committed suicide over the grave of his mistress.

The threat of war with Germany was short-lived

In the years 1881–84, Jules Ferry, the Foreign Minister, had co-operated with the Germans during a crucial period of colonial expansion, thus avoiding a conflict between the two countries. Ferry fell from office in 1885, and Boulanger's call for a war of revenge ended the entente between France and Germany. Anti-German agitation in Russia, a crisis in the Near East and the sabre rattling of Boulanger made the prospect of a new war, perhaps with Russia as an ally, a distinct possibility. A French frontier official, called Schnaebele, was arrested by the Germans, accused of spying, and this could have become the pretext for a conflict in April 1887. However, the crisis subsided, and effectively ended when Boulanger killed himself.

The Panama Scandal tarnished the Republic

Ferdinand de Lesseps, the engineer who had constructed the Suez Canal, floated a new company to build the Panama Canal in 1889. Three factors caused the project to fail: opposition to the canal by the US government, inhospitable climate and terrain, and financial mismanagement. In 1892, a legal case was brought against the company. Two investigations and two trials eventually revealed that two German Jewish financiers had spent two-thirds of all the company's funds in bribes to Republican politicians and journalists, and that the government had tried to cover up the corruption. Both at home and abroad, the reputation of the Republic was badly damaged.

The Dreyfus Case revealed the sharp divisions in French society

In 1894, a young French army officer was court-martialled and imprisoned for life on a charge of spying for the Germans. He was a Jew and a supporter of the Republic, two aspects of his character which were not popular amongst French army officers. In 1896, Colonel Picquart, Chief of Military Intelligence discovered that the documents Dreyfus was alleged to have written to the Germans were, in fact, forged by a Major Esterhazy. Colonel Picquart was removed from his post, and Esterhazy was tried, but acquitted, in 1898. When Republicans tried to make the army accept the new evidence, a group broadly known as Anti-Dreyfusards (monarchists, senior army officers, nationalists and anti-Semites) tried to use the case to discredit the republic. Republicans became convinced that Dreyfus was innocent. The novelist Emile Zola wrote a letter to the republican newspaper *L'Aurore* entitled 'J'accuse' in which he attacked and denounced several members of the French army. Esterhazy then confessed his guilt and Dreyfus was pardoned in 1899. However, he was kept out of the army and not fully reinstated as a major until 1906. The case itself was merely an excuse for an expression of support or criticism of the Republic, but the Republicans clearly won. Army reforms were then passed to prevent the exclusive influence of monarchists over the officer corps. Nevertheless, the army continued to believe it was separate from the Republic and claimed it had 'sanctity' from civilian interference.

Anti-clericalism was evidence of continuing divisions in French society

Despite anti-clerical legislation and resentment amongst the Catholic clergy towards the Republic, Pope Leo XIII tried to reconcile French Catholics to the new form of government. He aimed to disassociate the church from the monarchists. With this lead, Cardinal Lavigerie, Archbishop of Algiers, called on the citizens of France to 'rally' to the form of government under which they lived. Clerics began to support the Republic as a force for stability, although they were not all yet convinced. However, this *ralliement* (rallying) was destroyed by the Dreyfus Case. The Catholic clergy sided with the Anti-Dreyfusards. The republicans responded with equal hostility. A number of measures were passed: The Association Law (1901) prevented any religious organisation from existing without government approval. Monastic orders were expelled. The state introduced a monopoly over education (1904) and dictated that all religious teaching must cease after ten years. The Concordat of 1801 was cancelled (1905). This had given the state the right to make appointments in the clergy and paid the salaries of the church in return. Church property was to be retained by the clergy but its administration was placed in the hands of elected parish corporations. The Pope's reaction was to forbid the clergy of France from obeying the law of 1905. Tensions remained but gradually there was reconciliation on both sides, and the laws against monastic orders were relaxed. By 1914, some Catholic schools had reopened.

The Republic failed to meet the aspirations of the workers

The concern with the threat from the right wing delayed Republicans from dealing with more pressing social issues such as unemployment, health and housing. The Republican politicians represented the propertied middle classes who wanted to maintain the *status quo*. In 1906, Georges Clemenceau formed a government with a seventeen-point programme of reform. Yet the programme was never fully implemented. Too many politicians felt the issues were unimportant. However, the reaction of the workers was sometimes violent. From 1906, a series of riots and strikes rocked French industry. The government reacted firmly. On one occasion in 1910 during a rail strike, the Premier, Auguste Briande, called up the Reserves, thus enrolling most of the strikers into the armed forces where they were subject to military discipline. The reforms that did get through were the Workmen's Compensation Act (1898), the Ten Hours Factory Act (1906) and the Old Age Pensions Law (1910). By 1900, the numbers of workers organisations had increased, but they did not achieve as much as they might because of mutual antagonism and rivalry. Amongst the radicals, two main groups could be identified: the revisionist socialists and the revolutionaries.

The revisionists and the revolutionaries were an internal threat

Revolutionary socialists argued that any co-operation with the bourgeois government was pointless. Drawn from Marxists and the main trade union movement, the CGT (*Confédération Générale du Travail*), the revolutionaries aimed to use the strike, boycott and sabotage to bring down the Republic. In particular, Georges Sorel advocated the creation of a federated trade unionism to replace parliamentary democracy. His theories, published in *Reflexions sur la Violence* (1908), popularised the concept of Syndicalism. This was the use of a general strike, by all workers at the same time, to topple the government. Whilst unions had considered strike action to force concessions from employers over hours and pay, few had really thought about the general strike as a political weapon. By contrast, moderate socialists, who had formed a parliamentary party in 1880 under the leadership of Jules Guesde rejected violence. Guesde tended to preach violence but he was not popular, being dubbed the 'Red Jesuit'. Although the party was initially weak, in 1905 it was led by Guesde's rival, Jean Jaures, and began to gain influence over the government. Indeed, Aristide Briand and Viviani joined the government in 1906 and helped to implement reforms for workers. However, just at that moment, the radical CGT launched a strike wave in leading cities, in postal services, the wine trade and on the railways. The National Assembly debated a number of reforms but few were passed and Georges Clemenceau (the Premier) fell back on the army to control violent demonstrations. There were a number of deaths at Courrieres, Raon-l'Etape and Draveil, but the Republic survived.

Foreign policy

The loss of Alsace and Lorraine was a source of great anger

The loss of the two border provinces in 1871 was known as 'war in perpetuity' to the French, and many on the right thirsted for a war of *revanche* (revenge). There were war scares with Germany in 1875 and 1887, but also great bitterness over the Zabern Affair (1913). Relations remained bad and when France allied with Russia in 1894, and prevented any *rapprochement* (reconciliation) between Russia and Germany.

An alliance with Russia ended French isolation and changed Europe

In the 1880s, some groups in Russia and France were urging a common anti-German foreign policy. The Tsar was suspicious of republican and democratic France, preferring to remain on good terms with the Kaiser. However, in March 1890 the German refusal to renew the Reinsurance Treaty, changed the Russians attitude. Bismarck's decision to refuse to accept Russian securities (bonds) in return for financial loans, gave the French the opportunity to court the Russians. France gave money for famine relief in 1891, funded (with Belgium) much of the Trans-Siberian Railway in 1895 and assisted the Russians to purchase arms and fund infrastructural developments. Faced by the common colonial rivalry of Britain and the Triple Alliance (German, Austria, Italy) in central Europe, an entente in 1891 provided France and Russia with 'joint consultation' in the event of a 'threat to peace'. The Franco-Russian Alliance terms were then developed in 1894. Each country would aid the other if attacked by one or more other powers. The alliance was of great significance: France was no longer isolated in Europe and the balance of power had shifted away from Germany.

Relations with Britain improved after 1898

Britain and France had been colonial rivals for decades but relations had reached their nadir in 1898 at Fashoda. A small detachment of French marines, operating independently of the government, claimed the Sudan as French territory even though the British were already in occupation. War seemed imminent between the two countries. However, the French government feared the consequences of this in Europe. Both Britain and France shared a common concern with the aggressiveness of Germany, and the growth of a new German battle fleet after 1898. Delcassé, the Foreign Minister, hoped for closer relations with Britain, so, after the visit of Edward VII to Paris, an *entente cordiale* (friendly understanding) was concluded. This was not an alliance, and the agreement merely settled differences over the colonies. Britain was given a free hand in its sphere of influence in East Africa in return for a French free hand in Morocco, where a protectorate was to be set up if the existing government collapsed. Disputes over Newfoundland, Madagascar and Siam were settled.

The overseas Empire: colonialism and its effect on domestic politics

Rapid population growth in Germany alarmed the French because of the manpower potential for their armies. Without allies before 1894, France sought a colonial empire in Africa and the Far East with which to augment its strength. Jules Ferry tried to justify the colonial expansion as acquiring resources for French industry, but little of value was ever gained. Catholics were enthusiastic missionaries (75 per cent of all missionaries were French). Yet the most important reason for imperialism was prestige. The loss of Alsace-Lorraine and the continuing humiliation of military weakness drove France to acquire colonies. As a result, the population of the French Empire grew from 3 million to 60 million in the period 1870–1914. Yet the process was not smooth. Socialists refused to support the colonial policy and Jules Ferry's government was toppled in 1885 when a detachment of troops was defeated in Tonkin (Indo-China). Clemenceau regarded colonialism as 'high treason' and there were many who felt resources could be better deployed against Germany. However, the defeat of Italy in Abyssinia in 1896 produced an unexpected benefit for France. The Italians, whilst maintaining their alliance with Germany and Austria, concluded a secret alliance with France in 1902, promising never to go to war. This ended a period of intense rivalry that had begun after the French occupation of Tunis in 1881. France was thus free to concentrate on its German frontier.

Historical controversies

The Commune, at the birth of the republic, has generated considerable controversy

Was it a genuinely revolutionary movement, the crushing of which led to decades of bourgeois domination of France? Or was it simply a spasm of anger by Parisians in the wake of months of hardship? Karl Marx certainly attributed to it all the characteristics of proletarian revolution, but according to David Thomson and Theodore Zeldin, the Commune had its roots in a far older radical tradition so the 'modernity' of the uprising, fitting all the principles of Marxist doctrine, is a myth. F. Jellinek argued that, as a leaderless and incoherent outburst, it was 'fertile in examples of every revolutionary hypothesis'. The results of the Commune have been the source of dispute too. Most historians would argue that the Commune and its suppression lowered the prestige of the republic. J.P.T. Bury, by contrast, suggested that the traditional problem of governing Paris had been successfully resolved. Zeldin argues that Thiers was responsible for the Commune by moving the government from Paris, which he did, deliberately to force a showdown with the Parisians. Thomson is more accommodating about Thiers, believing that, like Abraham Lincoln, a civil war was necessary to preserve national unity, especially in the face of a greater foreign threat.

The Dreyfus Case broke the power of the anti-republicans

The Dreyfus Case is a classic example of the divisions that rent French society. The ideological divide between right and left was clear cut, although Jules Guesde called the affair, a 'civil war of the bourgeoisie'. The debates absorbed the French and delayed much needed progress on social reform, but it was a victory for republicanism in the end. The church and the army were discredited by their stubborn defence and there were far reaching reforms as a result.

Why, despite the divisions, did the Republic last so long?

Compared with régimes before, and with its eventual collapse under Nazi attack in 1940, the Third Republic lasted a long time. David Thomson argues that this was due to the ability to combine a conservative political structure with a radical social agenda. It reconciled the conservative and revolutionary traditions in France. However, Jean Pierre Azema and Michel Winock have suggested that the narrow basis of middle class support led to the stagnation of the Republic. F. Goguel believed the period was marked by a contest between the forces of the established order against the policies of movement. J. Chastenet sees the divisions as exaggerations: the moderate socialists and radicals should be praised for working with the Republic rather than against it. Marxist historians, such as H. Guillemin, always followed Marx's own assessment, which vigorously denounced the whole bourgeois edifice as one built on the corpses of the Communards. Beyond politics, historians such as Eugen Weber believe that this period was an important one in the modernisation of France. Communications, educational reform, the breakdown of parochialism and the development of a sense of nationhood were all far more significant. Theodore Zeldin went beyond even this assessment, examining in minute detail the deeper social and psychological basis of France, with all its divisions and changes. Perhaps the longevity of the Republic can be explained as the failure to produce alternatives and a balance of power between competing groups. In the end, all parties could see the need to continue to work with the Republic because the other consequences were unthinkable.

Tutorial

Progress questions

1. How successful were republican efforts to stabilise France between 1877 and 1914?

2. Why has so much controversy surrounded the Paris Commune?

3. With what justification can the Third Republic be described as a *bourgeois* régime?

4. How successful was the foreign policy of the Third Republic from 1871 to 1912?

Discussion points

1. Was the chief weakness of France in the period 1870–1914 the divided nature of its society, or were there other, more important factors?

2. Why did radicals and revolutionaries achieve so little in the period 1871–1914?

Practical assignment

Compile a list of social divisions, economic problems and political crises on one side of a page and then, on the other, list in each case how the Republic manage to overcome its problems. How well do these incidents reveal the strength of the regime?

Study and revision tips

1. Most questions about France in this period are concerned with how the Republic managed to survive at all. Examine this question carefully. Make sure you can show both the problems the Republic faced and its successful solutions.

2. Note how historians differ about the nature of the Republic. Try to include these views and be prepared to give the alternative arguments.

3

Germany: The Second Reich

One-minute summary – Germany was unified through war and the rapid victories the country enjoyed helped cement popular loyalty towards the new régime. However, Germany had a 'sham democracy', and too much power was concentrated in the hands of the Kaiser and his élites. Bismarck, the Chancellor, steered the parties of the *Reichstag*, altering his policies to win their support or to fit in with his own designs. In 1890, Germany adopted a 'new course' when Bismarck resigned and the young Kaiser Wilhelm II took over. The Kaiser's aggressive and impetuous diplomacy made him many enemies abroad, whilst his policy of trying to win over the workers largely failed. As a result, he and the élites began to consider more radical and belligerent solutions.

In this chapter you will learn:

▶ how the Franco-Prussian War led to the unification of Germany
▶ how Bismarck controlled German affairs between 1871–1890
▶ the nature of Germany under Kaiser Wilhelm II
▶ how German foreign policy laid the foundations for the Great War.

The Franco-Prussian War and the unification of Germany

In 1866, after lengthy negotiations, Prussia had become the leading element in the North German Confederation, a new political and military alliance that rivalled Austria as the dominant power in central Europe. The victory over Austria in 1866 made Bismarck popular, especially amongst liberals and those conservatives who had opposed the war at the beginning. Bennigsen became the leader of the National Liberals and he personally backed Bismarck until 1878. In return, he hoped that the achievement of a unified Germany (a liberal aim) would soon be followed by greater democracy. Bismarck claimed in his memoirs that he planned the unification of Germany from 1862, but, whilst he certainly intended to unite Germany under Prussian leadership through 'blood and iron' (war), he had to use his skill and adapt his policies to the situation. Eventually he managed to engineer a war with France, and made Napoleon III appear as the aggressor. This allowed him to invoke the support of the southern German states through a military alliance concluded in August 1866. It also enabled him to gain international sympathy. This kept France isolated and other powers, like Britain, neutral. Helmut von Moltke skilfully led the combined German forces, and France was defeated.

Figure 2. Germany in 1870.

Unification was achieved through war, popular enthusiasm and negotiation

As late as 1869, there was every indication that Bavaria and Württemberg, two of the southern states, would remain hostile to incorporation in a Prussian dominated Germany. Election results showed anti-Prussian sentiment was strong. Yet, the victory over France produced waves of nationalist enthusiasm. Bismarck used this against each of his opponents. He suggested that rulers might be overthrown if they resisted the will of the people and therefore the southern states dropped their territorial claims. Bavaria was won over by offering prestige concessions; it was the Bavarian king who suggested that the King of Prussia, Wilhelm (who was actually against being made German emperor), be called '*Deutscher Kaiser*'. The princes agreed to the title and Germany was unified on 18 January 1871 in the Palace of Versailles.

Bismarck, 1871-1890

The political structure of the Second *Reich* favoured authoritarianism

Bismarck created a federal system that was dominated in every respect by Prussia and the Prussian king. As he was the Chancellor of Prussia, he was elevated to the Chancellorship of Germany. Prussia had 17 out of 58 votes in upper house and made up three fifths of the territory of Germany. Prussia's King was the emperor by hereditary right. The *Reichstag* (Lower House) could only delay laws/taxes, even though it was democratically elected by almost universal manhood suffrage. The liberals had hoped for more and would aim to pressure Bismarck into further concessions in the future. The *Bundesrat* (Upper House) controlled legislation; each member represented a state's government and not the people. It could dissolve the *Reichstag* and it could, with the emperor's approval, declare war. Thus the upper house, like the chancellor, was not answerable to the *Reichstag* or the people, only to the monarchy. The monarch had powers to appoint ministers, direct foreign policy, and influence domestic policy through the chancellor, but Wilhelm I tended to leave affairs to Bismarck.

Divided political groups enabled Bismarck to divide and rule

The Conservatives were drawn from the Protestant aristocracy of the north (the *Junkers*). They believed in protectionism and lived on rents earned from land. Land was falling in value at the end of the nineteenth century and so the *Junkers* wanted to raise tariffs against food imports to keep German agriculture profitable. The Catholic Centre Party was made up of men from all classes, but its support came mainly from south and the Rhineland. The Centre Party believed in resisting centralisation, wanted social reform and more 'constitutional' government (that is, less autocracy). Bismarck thought they weren't patriotic, but this was unfounded. The National Liberals were founded on the educated and wealthy middle class, and they were in favour of centralisation, constitutional government, and free trade. They declined after 1877 as protectionists became more powerful in government. The Left Liberals were similar to the National Liberals but took an anti-militarist, anti-state and radical approach to politics, demanding greater social reform. The Social Democratic Party (SPD) was formed in 1869, and grew rapidly. It was popular with the working classes in towns for its radical, anti-authoritarian agenda (but it enjoyed less support in the south). Its members were often harassed by the police. Finally foreign minorities aimed to split away from the German *Reich* but were largely ignored.

Bismarck's plans were to centralise power

Bismarck needed legislation to make Germany more centralised, so he initially co-operated with the National Liberals (the largest party in *Reichstag* in 1871). He unified the army, civil service, railways, postal service, legal systems, currency, and imposed laws, language and customs on foreign minorities. He then concentrated his efforts on trying to suppress internal opposition. He felt the foreign minorities, SPD and Catholics were the threats to unity and centralisation. Bismarck had to create a sense of national identity which did not exist (except for a handful of intellectuals). Many Germans were still proud of belonging to a region (such as Bavaria), a phenomenon known as 'particularism'.

Bismarck tried to suppress his opponents in the *Kulturkampf*

Catholics had wanted to see the German speaking parts of Austria included in a greater Germany (called *Grossdeutschland*) in 1871. This would have meant there would have been more Catholics to oppose the Protestants of the north. Bismarck was looking for a way of breaking their influence. Pope Pius IX had issued a bull of Papal Infallibility which stated that the Pope's word could not be opposed. Some German Catholics had rejected it and Bismarck stepped in to support them when they were ejected from the Church. He hoped to make it an issue of national loyalty, but predictably most Catholics in Germany backed the Pope. When Germany was later unified, southern Catholics feared persecution from the Protestants of the north and had formed the Catholic Centre Party. The party attracted the support of all Catholics across Germany including the Polish and French minorities. Consequently Bismarck felt that the Catholics might be the leading element of a whole movement against German unity. After all, Prussia's enemies had been Catholic Austria and Catholic France in 1866 and 1870, so foreign intervention could not be ruled out. Bismarck's strategy was to link up with Russia (its Orthodox Church hated the Catholic Church), to encourage anti-clericalism in Italy by his own examples of anti-clerical legislation to suppress Catholics in Germany, and to encourage support from the Protestant National Liberals and other secular groups.

The progress of the 'struggle for culture'

In 1872, Bismarck severed diplomatic relations with the Vatican, and expelled Jesuits. The following year he passed the May Laws (with the state appointment of priests in schools, greater controls of the coercive measures priests who taught could use, and the use of secular inspectors in schools). In 1875 civil marriage was made compulsory. Religious orders (such as the Benedictines) were dissolved. The Pope condemned the measures as 'null and void'. The effect of the laws was that support for Catholic Centre Party increased and they gained more seats in the Reichstag. Before long, a third of the German people were angry at the régime. Far from unifying Germany against the Church, Bismarck was dividing it.

Bismarck was forced to change his policy

Bismarck knew he was antagonising the Catholics, but there was no way to reverse the policy without losing face. However, the appointment of a new Pope (Leo XIII) in 1878 allowed negotiations to re-open. Yet there were other pressures on Bismarck that compelled him to make the change. The SPD had gained 0.5 million votes in 1877 and Bismarck feared this new threat. Moreover, Catholic Austria was considering an alliance with Germany and the *Kulturkampf* stood in the way of this arrangement. In addition, as Bismarck had decided to protect the German economy and imposed protection, it had cost him the support of the National Liberals. He could not oppose both the Catholic Centre Party and National Liberals at the same time. The Catholics seemed to support protectionism which offered Bismarck the chance to form a new conservative alliance. So, in 1879, an agreement was reached with the Catholics: Berlin was to be informed of all appointments in the Catholic Church of Germany, and in return Catholics would agree not to oppose the government. As a result, Bismarck began to revoke the May Laws.

Protectionism was necessary but also served political purposes

Before 1870, agriculture was dominant in Germany, although Prussia had some areas of industrialisation. Unification made it possible for infrastructure to develop and for an 'economy of scale' to be developed. In 1875, France paid a war indemnity that was used to support German industry. Financial speculators also backed industrial development projects and invested widely. Consequently, there was an economic boom caused by industrialisation. However, at the same time, cheap food from Russia (rye), Austria and the United States (wheat) threatened the competitiveness of German agriculture. In 1879, Bismarck imposed tariffs on foreign food and other products to protect the German economy. This was popular amongst the middle classes, particularly those engaged in manufacturing. Economists believed Germany could continue to develop under protectionism. It could become more self-sufficient. Bismarck saw political benefits too. Under free trade, taxes were raised for the government's revenue and it had to seek the approval of the *Reichstag*. With tariffs it did not have to rely so much on the lower house. This gave Bismarck the chance to finally break with the National Liberals who were demanding more power sharing. He aimed to get the support of the Catholics and conservatives against the Social Democrats (SPD) and liberals.

Bismarck attacked socialism

Socialists opposed monarchy, the army, autocracy, private property, and private ownership of the land. Bismarck not only held these values dear, but saw international socialism as an attack on patriotism and his policy of authoritarian centralisation. Two assassination attempts against Kaiser Wilhelm I gave Bismarck his excuse to suppress the SPD in 1879. The Exceptional Law (1879) outlawed the Socialist Party, whilst societies, meetings and publications were banned. The police could deport suspects. Trade unions were declared illegal. During this suppression, Bismarck blamed socialists for the downturn in the economy in the 1880s. Yet his policy was more sophisticated than blatant repression. He planned to win over the workers, away from the socialists, with a policy 'state socialism'. Compulsory insurance for sickness at work (1883), against accidents (1884) and pensions for the disabled and elderly (1889) were designed to make the public feel that socialism was unnecessary. However, the German socialists grew in popularity. Groups met in secret or abroad, and accepted their exile (like Karl Marx, who worked in London). In 1890, support for the SPD grew to 1.5 million votes. This indicates that the government was not keeping pace with the aspirations of the public.

Bismarck's foreign policy was to preserve a German balance of power

In 1871, to reassure international opinion, Bismarck declared 'Germany is satiated', suggesting that there would be no further territorial expansion. Bismarck's aim was to preserve German hegemony in central Europe by a skilful balancing act of diplomacy between the other countries. He stated: 'Germany should try to be *à trois* in a world governed by five powers'.

Bismarck's aims in the 1870s

▶ Remain at peace (so as to develop the country internally).

▶ Maintain the new balance of power (with Germany dominant in central Europe).

▶ Avoid Russia and Austria clashing in Balkans which might draw in Germany.

▶ Resolve the Eastern question crises before they led to war (1878 to 1886).

▶ Keep France isolated, to prevent war of revenge over Alsace-Lorraine.

▶ Prevent an anti-German coalition by keeping on good terms with other Great Powers.

▶ Consider a secondary aim of acquiring colonies. He did this under popular pressure because he saw no benefit in colonies, but saw the advantage of marshalling popular support. He said: 'My map of Africa lies in Europe'.

The legacy of unification methods influenced his foreign policy

Bismarck used military force to achieve his aims and he maintained a strong army in Germany. During the unification, he isolated each of his opponents in turn, Denmark, Austria and France, by skilful diplomacy. He aimed to keep France isolated after 1871 as she was the main threat. Bismarck had tried to plan ahead but probably seized opportunities, or created them where he could. His military victories stirred national enthusiasm. Later, Wilhelm II and his advisors saw Bismarckian tactics as a way to generate patriotism and thus stave off socialism. The liberals tended to support their country, and forget their criticisms, when the nation's security was at stake. Thus the hallmarks of Bismarck's foreign policy were to threaten war, to maintain strong military forces, to isolate opponents and to maintain a diplomatic balance (with Germany as the 'honest broker') as crises emerged. Having redrawn the map of Europe, Bismarck seemed anxious to preserve it the way it was.

The *Dreikaiserbund* was a conservative alliance

The evidence of the conservative nature of Germany's policy was evident when Bismarck arranged for the meeting of the Three Emperors (Austria's Franz Josef, Russia's Alexander II, and Germany's Wilhelm I) in 1872. They concluded an informal alliance to preserve the European *status quo*, especially in the Balkans. It was designed to keep France isolated. She would not act against all three. It represented conservative principles in Europe; all wanted to resist the progressive politics of Britain and France. It also followed the conservative pattern of the earlier Holy Alliance of 1815 (set up to resist revolutions). In 1873, military agreements followed between each member and in 1881, these agreements were formalised. They were renewed in 1884 but lapsed in 1887, so Bismarck quickly concluded the Reinsurance Treaty with Russia.

The 'fatherland in danger war scare' (1875) was to keep France isolated

The chance that there might be war in 1875 illustrates the poor relations between France and Germany. France recovered rapidly from the defeat of 1871, paying off the war indemnity, and passing new army laws. German army officers discussed 'preventive war' to stop the French from initiating a war of revenge. Bismarck also feared that a monarchist revival in France might mean an alliance between France and Austria or Italy. Moreover, the *Kulturkampf* was angering Catholics in Germany, Belgium and France. When Bismarck's army bill was being opposed in the Reichstag, it looked as if his policy was failing. To generate enthusiasm for the government, Bismarck played on nationalist sentiments. He sent delegates to Russia to defend the idea of preventive war, halted the export of horses to Belgium (a sign of war), and (secretly) submitted an article to the press called 'Is War in Sight?' His bill was passed amid panic. Decazes, the French Foreign Minister, told *The Times* that Germany wanted to 'bleed France white'. With war possible, Britain and Russia demanded to know why there was a warlike atmosphere in Berlin. Bismarck was forced to concede that there was no threat of war; it was a 'storm in a teacup'. The crisis had served Bismarck's purposes but it showed that France could utilise Russian and British support and was perhaps not as isolated as it seemed. Bismarck sought a solution.

The Dual Alliance, 1879, gave Germany a firm ally to keep France isolated

During Russia's war against the Ottoman Empire in 1877–78, relations between Austria and Russia became strained. Bismarck felt he could not remain neutral and decided to side with Austria in a formal alliance, although he tried to give the appearance of neutrality at the Berlin Congress (June 1878), a settlement which ended this Near Eastern Crisis. Relations with Russia deteriorated when the Dual Alliance was concluded. The terms were secret which meant that Tsar Alexander II thought it was a 'coalition against Russia' and Russian troops gathered on the border in Poland. This confirmed Bismarck's belief that the Russians were too unpredictable to make reliable alliance partners. Policies there depended on who was influential at court, but Austria was a more predictable partner. To win over the conservatives and Catholics at home, against the National Liberals and the SPD, he hoped an alliance with Austria would be welcomed, perhaps as a prelude to the formation of a Greater Germany. In fact, Bismarck wanted to preserve the Habsburg Empire as it was: too many Catholic Germans (that is, former Austrians) would upset Prussian domination of Germany. Bismarck was also afraid of an Austro-Russian alliance against Germany. His Dual Alliance would prevent one. Erich Eyck argued that Bismarck also wanted to win over Britain. The *Dreikaiserbund* was a threat to the British, and that might drive them towards France. By avoiding a direct commitment to Russia, the British would be more reassured and France would remain isolated.

The alliance terms favoured Austria

Andrassy, the Austrian Foreign Minister, knew Bismarck wanted Austrian support. Germany was committed to assisting Austria, but Austria merely had to remain neutral (if a war broke out with France). However, both would help each other if there was a war with Russia. Yet, the Kaiser knew there was a weakness in antagonising Russia. Bismarck's substitutes of Italy (1882) and Romania (1883) hardly made up for the loss of Russia as a partner. Consequently, the Kaiser called the Dual Alliance a '*partie inégale*' because Germany *had* to support Austria, but Austria could observe a 'benevolent neutrality' if France went to war. The Dual Alliance was, in fact, unnecessary for Germany. Russia had stated in September 1879, that it would be neutral if France went to war. After 1879, in the face of the Dual Alliance, it was more likely to look upon France as an ally. Indeed, Bismarck, and his successors, were forced to support Austria's interests in the Balkans against Russia. Moreover, the secret nature of the clauses merely encouraged other powers to adopt secret diplomacy. This increased suspicion and made war more likely.

Bismarck responded by making other arrangements

Bismarck concluded formal clauses to the *Dreikaiserbund* in 1881. This provided for consultation if any of them sought change in the Balkans or Near East. Each power was to be neutral and localise any conflicts in the region. As a result, Russia saw the *Dreikaiserbund* as a useful lever against Britain. Romania grew fearful of Russian ambitions and concluded an alliance with Austria, and therefore with Germany. To continue to further its interests in the Balkans, Austria concluded a secret treaty with Serbia (against Russian influence in Bulgaria).

Bismarck had to make more changes in light of the Bulgarian Crisis 1885–86

The Bulgarians rejected overbearing Russian interference in their affairs following the successful rebellion of Eastern Roumelia against Ottoman rule in 1885, where it had been demonstrated that Bulgarians could act independently. Russian attempts to hold on to their influence in the region brought them into conflict with Austria in 1886. Bismarck therefore decided to renew his link with Russia in a separate alliance called the Reinsurance Treaty in 1887. The Russian press had been very anti-German and some papers advocated an alliance with France instead. This could mean that Bismarck had been forced to do something to forestall a potential Franco-Russian alliance. The terms of the Reinsurance Treaty were that war with a third power meant neutrality for either Russia or Germany. It was stressed that attempts should be made to localise any war. Bismarck also agreed to support Russia in her attempts to see influence restored in Bulgaria. The alliance would be void if either attacked another power. Bismarck hoped this treaty would keep Russia from attacking Austria.

Verdicts on the Reinsurance Treaty are unfavourable

The Reinsurance Treaty did not actually conflict with the Dual Alliance as long as Germany was not the aggressor. Germany would decide which side to support. However, the secretive nature of the Treaty left a feeling of bitterness when it was revealed in 1896. Relations between Russia and Germany also remained bad despite the treaty. Moreover, because the existence of the Reinsurance Treaty gave the Austrians cause to doubt the sincerity of the Germans, Berlin had to go to considerable lengths to reassure them in the years that followed (and especially in 1914). The Tsar kept the Reinsurance Treaty secret because of the anti-German feeling in Russia.

Verdict on Bismarck's foreign policy: success, but problems for the future

Bismarck was a skilful diplomat. He tried to make the other powers dependent on Germany. He had a good understanding of the interests of other powers and he appealed to these interests. However, Bismarck failed to gain security from France. There was a threat that she would launch a war of revenge (*revanche*) and Bismarck failed to find a solution to Austro-Russian rivalry in the Balkans. He tried to remain on good terms with them both. Although he did not want colonies, he gave way to popular pressure and acquired parts of Africa and Asia. This led to rivalry with Britain which worsened after he resigned in 1890.

There is a way to understand Bismarck's motives

Bismarck wanted to avoid a war on two fronts. This meant keeping France and Russia apart. He saw the world locked in a struggle between order (autocracy) and revolution (the Left across Europe, Republican France). He felt that France was unlikely to get an ally whilst she remained a Republic, particularly while he sought allies who represented order. He felt Britain's system made her unstable (it had many changes of government), and Italy's made her weak. These points would explain his revival of the Holy Alliance and his other alliances with conservative powers. They also explain why Bismarck told the Tsar that the Reinsurance Treaty was needed to avoid revolution in Europe (which would be inevitable if France defeated Germany in a war of revenge). Bismarck's foreign policy decisions were also affected by his domestic policy: Catholics were needed in Germany, which led to the Dual Alliance, and the 'fatherland in danger' crisis was used to outflank liberals in the Reichstag.

Wilhelmine Germany, 1890–1914

Bismarck's resignation represented a change of course for Germany

Kaiser Wilhelm I died in 1888, and his liberal son Frederick III died the same year. Wilhelm II, the new Kaiser, was only 21. He was ambitious and determined. His withered left arm was a source of humiliation to him and some have speculated that he was forever trying to compensate for his physical deformity by acts which he thought would make him popular. Bismarck wanted to continue in control, but Wilhelm wanted more colonies, a larger navy, the end of the Russian alliance and closer relations with Great Britain (he was a grandson of Queen Victoria). Wilhelm also wanted to end the anti-socialist legislation, hoping to make himself popular with the common people. Above all, Wilhelm wanted to rule as absolute monarch, without Bismarck's interference. When Bismarck disagreed with the young Kaiser, *Punch* famously recorded the resignation in a cartoon by Tenniel as 'dropping the pilot'.

The new course: what changed?

Bismarck had wanted limited aims in foreign affairs: security against attack and a focus on Europe. By contrast, Wilhelm wanted an unlimited 'world policy' called *Weltpolitik*, meaning broadly, 'Germany's interests were everywhere'. Wilhelm wanted a more powerful nation but in doing so he upset the balance of power and therefore jeopardised Germany's security.

Naval expansion was designed to give Germany an empire overseas

In 1890, Wilhelm wanted to see an expansion of the German navy. He believed that Britain's imperial success was due to the Royal Navy and he wanted to emulate that success. This idea coincided with the work of Alfred T. Mahan, an American, who came to the conclusion that naval strength always ensured imperial expansion. In 1895, the Kiel Canal was opened. This connected the North Sea and the Baltic. It was large enough to accommodate the largest warships. In 1897, Admiral Tirpitz advocated naval expansion to give Germany the ability to protect German colonial, economic and diplomatic interests. The first naval law was passed in 1898. There were other laws for expansion of the German fleet in 1900 (when the Germans had wanted to influence the Boer War against Britain but couldn't), in 1906 (after a new warship design was revealed), in 1908 (in light of British naval expansion) and in 1912 (after the Kaiser's War Council had decided to go to war).

Britain responded to the arms race with Germany

After 1903, Britain was concerned about German naval expansion. Germany already had Europe's most formidable army, but aggressive naval expansion appeared menacing. Tirpitz had announced that he wanted a navy so large, that even Britain would hesitate before attacking it. The Royal Navy formed a new fleet at Rosyth to cover the North Sea and, for the first time, plans were drawn up to fight Germany. In 1905 Britain began work on a new design of battleship, the Dreadnought. It rendered all other types of ship obsolete. The Germans were working on their own version when the Royal Navy launched the vessel in 1906. Tirpitz feared that the British would produce these new ships more quickly than Germany and perhaps launch a pre-emptive strike (to 'Copenhagen' the German fleet). The first German Dreadnought (or 'capital ship') was laid down in 1907. The British government tried to slow down the arms race, but it failed due to public pressure in Britain in 1909 and German intransigence at a conference in 1912. Tirpitz reasoned that, as France and Britain were co-operating closely, Germany should be allowed to build a fleet comparable to them both.

The effects of the naval building programme were far reaching

The failure of the talks was critical. Britain and France secretly agreed to realign their fleets (Britain to defend the North Sea and Channel, France to concentrate on the Mediterranean). Germany was therefore convinced that Britain would have to be defeated in war. The 'War Council' was held in 1912 to discuss how to do it. The Kaiser wanted immediate action, but Tirpitz obtained a delay of 18 months to prepare the German fleet for war. Historian Volker Berghahn wrote that the arms race was the primary cause of the First World War. P.J Bartlett disagrees, arguing that it was not inevitable at all. Whatever its international effect, the expense of building the German fleet diverted resources that could have been spent on the domestic economy.

German colonialism was the driving force of *Weltpolitk*

Wilhelm's drive for colonies in the 1890s antagonised other European powers. The Kaiser believed that the Germans (the Aryans) were the dominating race of the world because of their history, racial characteristics, great artists and philosophers, and leaders (like himself). *Weltpolitik* referred to global influence in colonial matters, but may have also hinted at world domination. In the Kaiser's imagination, great swathes of the world would be run by German administrators, just as the British were then doing. Wilhelm's methods for achieving this great object were disturbing. He broke the protocols of diplomacy by his dramatic gestures. In 1896, when Europe was horrified by Turkish massacres of Armenian rebels, Wilhelm sent a signed photograph of himself to show support to the Turks. In 1898, he toured the Near East like a conqueror (especially on his visit to Jerusalem). He sent military advisors to the Turkish army. He wanted a railway built between Berlin and Baghdad which would draw trade away from the maritime routes (dominated by Britain) or the continental overland routes (through Russia). Rumours circulated that the Kaiser wanted to create an empire in the Near East. His officials pretended that the Kaiser favoured conversion to Islam.

The Kaiser had ambitions in the Far East and North Africa

Wilhelm ordered the seizure of Kiaochow in China as 'compensation' for Russia's annexation of Port Arthur. In the suppression of the Chinese Boxer rebellion (1900), it is alleged he remarked 'Go! And act like Huns' to demonstrate German racial superiority and ruthlessness. In 1906, he angered European statesmen by his behaviour at the Algeçiras Conference (1906). He sent the gunboat *Panther* to Morocco in 1911 to protect 'German interests', although no one could define what those interests were. They were probably little more than the Kaiser's belief that he should be consulted on matters of international importance. It was in the 1910s that Wilhelm began to refer to himself as the 'All Highest'.

Relations with Russia deteriorated

Wilhelm refused to renew the Reinsurance Treaty with Russia in 1890. This may have been to pursue closer relations with Britain (Russia's rival). It may have been logical since Germany was linked to Austria. Wilhelm certainly thought relations could be maintained with Russia at a personal level. However, he had been shocked to discover through secret despatches that Alexander III thought him a 'low type – not to be trusted'. The new Tsar, Nicholas II, and Wilhelm did enjoy close personal ties. However the Russian court was divided in its view of Germany. Relations gradually deteriorated because of German tariffs against Russian grain in 1902, a refusal by German financiers to invest in the Trans-Siberian railway, German foreign policy in the Near East, and the Bosnian crisis (1908). In 1894, France and Russia concluded a secret alliance to assist each other in the event of a war with Germany.

Germany's internal political divisions made it a 'sham democracy'

In theory, Germany had a strong executive (Kaiser) but also a democratic system (elected *Reichstag*), but in practice the Kaiser was indecisive, unpredictable and wouldn't delegate. The Chancellor, Foreign Minister and Army were answerable to the Kaiser. Without direction, they evolved their own contradictory policies. The Kaiser had a group of advisors, adjutants, official and unofficial cabinets, and secret inner councils, none of whom were accountable to the Reichstag. Moreover, the Kaiser tended to make rash and dramatic statements which were taken as policy statements. In 1908, his conversation with a British army officer was printed in *The Telegraph,* which suggested the 'British are mad, relations are strained, and the German people dislike the British'. He hadn't taken any advice over the article and it caused an outcry both in Britain and in Germany. The *Bundesrat* generally supported Wilhelm because of the prospect of Germany's aggrandisement. The *Reichstag* was more critical, but did not have the power to offer alternatives. The general public were generally loyal to the Kaiser, but a number of right-wing pressure groups emerged to try to influence policy. These were the Agrarian League (1884), The German Colonial League (1882), The Pan-German League (formed in 1893, they wanted all German speakers in a greater Germany), and The Navy League (1898). All these groups shared a distaste for democracy.

Germany's domestic policy enjoyed a 'liberal phase' (1890–94)

The 'liberal' phase was the policy of Chancellor Caprivi (a former Prussian soldier). He first tackled the issue of tariffs by arranging commercial treaties with Austria, Italy, Spain, Romania, and Russia (1892–94). This made imports cheaper and therefore the price of food fell. It aroused opposition of landowners who pressured for protectionist reform through the Agrarian League. Caprivi also relaxed the anti-socialist laws. Some laws were abolished; industrial courts were set up (1890) to settle wage disputes, factory inspections were initiated (1891) and workers were given the right to negotiate working conditions. This was designed to wean workers away from socialism. However, criticisms reached the Kaiser. He was nicknamed the 'beggar's emperor' because he appeared to favour the common people. Wilhelm had wanted to create *Sammlungspolitik* (literally 'togetherness politics') and Caprivi had tried to create a 'consensus', but Wilhelm's pride could not stomach the insulting title it earned him.

Germany endured a more reactionary phase (1894–1914)

The two chancellors responsible for carrying out the Kaiser's new policies at home were Prince Hohenlohe (1894–1900) and Bülow (1900–1909). Hohenlohe was a conservative and, at 75, eager only to do as the Kaiser bid him. He was generally pro-Russian and favoured by the aristocratic right wing. Bülow was also an accommodating chancellor, earning himself the nickname 'the eel' for his ability to fit in with the Kaiser's, or others', whims. On tariffs, Bülow responded when the Alliance of Rye and Steel was formed; protectionists in agriculture and industrialists who wanted greater arms expenditure put pressure on the chancellor to re-impose high tariffs on grain from Russia in 1902. Conciliation to the workers also continued at the Kaiser's bidding. In 1903 a sickness insurance law was introduced. This had an impact on the SPD. Revisionists, led by Eduard Bernstein, called for a more co-operative policy with the government and the abandonment of revolutionary agendas from 1891. Support for the SPD continued to grow. In 1912 they became the largest party in the *Reichstag*. Hans-Ulrich Wehler argued that this forced the government to 'escape forwards', to plan for a war to reunite the nation with patriotism. The Kaiser was certainly alarmed by the rise of socialist support. He described a third of Germany as *Staatsfeinde* (enemies of the state). This included Jews, foreign minorities and even Catholics. After 1900, there was repression against the Poles and the French of Alsace-Lorraine.

The importance of Germany's economic development

Germany experienced rapid economic growth after 1871. This is illustrated by the figures below:

Urban population of Germany (total population in millions and % of total)

1890	1900	1914
5.6	8.7	14
11.3%	15.5%	21%

Levels of industrialisation per capita (compared with GB in 1900 index = 100)

1880	1900	1913
25	52	85

Britain's development in same period

87	100	115

Iron/steel production (millions of tonnes)

1890	1900	1913
4.1	6.3	17.6

Rapid industrialisation brought its own difficulties but the concomitant urbanisation and lack of political development stored up particular problems. One case example will illustrate the general problem.

Hamborn was a classic example of the effects of industrialisation

Hamborn was a Ruhr valley settlement which was engulfed by rapid development. It had a population of 4,200 in 1880, which rose to 102,000 in 1910. Migrant workers from the east, or from the rural community, found themselves living in substandard accommodation. The speed of residential construction often meant that social facilities were not constructed. The original inhabitants provided some of these, especially pubs. Unlike the slower development of British towns, where there was a mixture of classes in adjacent wards, these industrial towns were exclusively one class with sharp segregation from the middle class. The workers' areas tended to become the focus of shared hardships and solidarity. Until 1918, strikes were difficult to organise (paragraph 153 of the Industrial Code stated: 'forcing others to join a strike is a criminal offence') and in the period before the First World War wages were low. Support for the SPD in Hamborn was considerable.

It was thought that urbanisation had a negative effect on the loyalty of Germans

Town dwellers were regarded by the régime as likely suspects for socialist ideas. It was often thought rural folk were more patriotic, more conservative and healthier. Urban workers were less well nourished, able to share their protest at their conditions, and therefore able to form opposition groups in large numbers.

There may have been a fundamental flaw in German politics

Wehler argued that the SPD lacked experience in government, and that the defeat of the middle classes in the 1848 revolutions (in contrast to the British middle classes which secured power-sharing in 1832), caused a fatal weakness in German politics. The political system failed to develop along democratic lines as élites wanted to maintain power. Solutions offered by the two sides tended to be extreme: war, or revolution.

Militarism was a philosophy that affected much of German society
History taught the élites, and much of the German public, that military solutions
were glorious and successful. Germany had been unified by force of arms. Its
armies were thought to be invincible. Before the First World War, there were
paramilitary groups (such as Young Germany) and many veterans' associations
and military clubs. One sixth of German men belonged to these anti-democratic
and sometimes anti-Semitic groups. The influential writer Friedrich von
Bernhardi (*Germany and the Next War*, 1911) argued that war was the greatest
test of manhood and the 'fitness' of the state. The army had considerable influence
at court because of their numbers and the high esteem in which Wilhelm II held
them. When social problems seemed insoluble, the Kaiser turned to the army to
provide a quick solution.

The German army developed aggressive war plans
Until 1892, the General Staff planned for a war against Russia (in support of
Austria). After 1892, Count von Schlieffen, the Chief of Staff, assumed that Russia
and France would co-operate. His solution to the problem of a 'war on two fronts'
was to launch a knock-out blow against France before turning on Russia (which
mobilised slowly). The strategy was to envelop the French army. In 1905, von
Moltke altered the plan, weakening the proposed western attack, to reinforce the
exposed East Prussian border. In 1909, the General Staff promised to aid Austria
in all circumstances. This went beyond the alliance terms of 1879 without the
authority of the Foreign Ministry. The Kaiser reinforced this by announcing in
1908 and again in 1912 that Austria's call for support would be a 'command for
him'.

The relationship of the Kaiser and the army was revealed in the Zabern Affair
In 1913, ill-treatment of civilians at Zabern (Alsace) and the verbal abuse by a 20-
year-old lieutenant led to protests. Armed patrols roamed the streets. The
German press was critical of the army's swagger. A vote of no confidence was
passed in the Reichstag. The army held its own 'trial' and acquitted all the officers
involved. The middle classes supported the army. The affair revealed the
weaknesses of the Reichstag, the unconstitutional behaviour of the army, backed
by the Kaiser, and the 'consequences of social militarism' (Wehler).

Bethmann-Hollweg lacked the ability to avert a crisis
Bethmann-Hollweg became chancellor in 1909 when Bülow was dismissed as a
result of the *Daily Telegraph* Affair (page 36). Whilst skilful in domestic affairs,
Bethmann-Hollweg lacked any experience in foreign politics which is probably
why the Kaiser picked him. However, he failed to capitalise on Wilhelm's
unpopularity to force constitutional change and lacked the courage to oppose the
emperor's disastrous foreign policies. John Rohl argued that the Kaiser 'dictated
policy to an amazing extent ... all appointments, all bills, all diplomatic moves
were made on his orders.' This suggests, as Ralph Fleney noted, an 'invasion from

above', or greater interference that Bethmann-Hollweg would have found impossible to oppose. At the same time, the growth of the SPD in the Reichstag and the increasingly independent actions of the army and navy eroded the chancellor's position from below and denied him a counterpoise to the Kaiser's authority.

Relations with France and Russia were worsening prior to 1914

Alsace-Lorraine remained the stumbling block in relations with France and the Schlieffen plan assumed French hostility in the event of a war involving Russia. Russia seemed ever more likely to intervene in the Balkans in the years after a humiliating defeat against Japan in 1905. This only served to drive the Kaiser still closer to his ally Austria.

Anglo-German relations deteriorated between 1900 and 1914

In 1890 relations between Britain and Germany were good. Germany imported many British goods and it was thought that the end of the Reinsurance Treaty (revealed in 1896) would benefit Britain (as an anti-Russian attitude prevailed there). However the Kaiser wanted to make Germany greater than Britain. In 1893, Britain asked for support against France in a dispute over Siam. Germany refused and Britain reached an agreement with France. To the Kaiser, Britain appeared to be weak and therefore not a worthy ally. In 1896 Wilhelm sent a note (the Kruger telegram) to congratulate the Boers on defeating the British Jameson Raid. This angered Britons. The Kaiser also appeared to be interested in creating an empire in the Near East which might threaten British trade. The *Daily Telegraph* article and the Naval Race worsened relations. Germany also appeared to be threatening Britain's global trade. South America had been a region which purchased many British goods. In the 1910s, German manufacturers were 'dumping' mass produced goods at reduced prices to squeeze out their British competitors. Moreover, German manufacturing, especially heavy industrial output, was catching up with Britain.

Proposals for an alliance with Britain came to nothing

In 1898, Chamberlain had suggested an alliance. The Kaiser tactlessly informed the Tsar of the idea. The following year, Bülow and the Kaiser visited Britain. Chamberlain spoke of their common interests and the value of an alliance. It was criticised in Germany and Bülow used anti-British feelings in the Reichstag to pass naval laws. In 1901, when the Kaiser visited Queen Victoria, Chamberlain again suggested an alliance. However, Holstein effectively sabotaged the alliance proposals. It was generally felt that Germany already held the balance of power in Europe. Germany wanted security in the Balkans or Eastern Europe, but Britain could only offer naval strength and looked for colonial security. Britain badly wanted this security in the Far East against Japan (until 1902 when it allied) and the European powers there. The Kaiser was confident of good co-operation with the other powers and saw no need to defend Britain's weak position there.

Although Germany did not assist the Boers in the South African War (1899–1902), she did send arms, and the German people favoured the Boers. In 1912, naval talks broke down and Haldane (Secretary of State for War) made some aggressive remarks, as did Lloyd George after the Moroccan Crisis of that year. Finally, in the Germans' view, the Ententes with France and Russia put Britain beyond any alliance.

Revisionist views of German history

Hans-Ulrich Wehler argued, as one of a group of so-called 'young German historians', that domestic politics affected the Reich's foreign policies, and that there was a 'revolution from above', meaning the régime's élites looked for radical solutions to their problems. They sought to 'escape forwards' or use progressive ideas to maintain their own popularity. When this failed they resorted to war as a tool of popular politics. By contrast, Hans Rosenberg believed that economic interpretations were paramount. The economic depressions Germany faced caused changes in policies. Erich Eyck maintained that personalities were important, particularly Bismarck and Wilhelm II, if one was to understand the period. Since the 1960s, German historians sought to find the link between undemocratic politics in Germany and international relations. Georg Iggers was one of those who examined social history, such as the great social shifts in the urban-industrial regions like the Ruhr, as well as political history, to explain what happened. In addition, the recent debates on Nazi Germany have cast a long shadow over studies of Germany before 1914, because it has been alleged that German people had a pathological hatred of the Jews or harboured authoritarian views that lent themselves to Nazism. These views are still very controversial and there are significant weaknesses in trying to locate grievances and the anguish that resulted from the war and the Depression in the period before 1914.

Tutorial

Progress questions
1. 'Masterful and dominant' or 'irresponsible and misguided': which description best fits Bismarck after 1871 and Kaiser Wilhelm II after 1890?

2. How valid is the view that 'the domestic problems facing the rulers of Germany were primarily the result of social and economic change'?

3. How well was Germany served by its governments before 1914?

4. What principles guided Bismarck's foreign policy?

Discussion points
1. Discuss the two questions and responses below.

Did Bismarck plan the system of alliances after unification?
No, he seized opportunities and reacted to changes in international relations (such as the scramble for Africa, where he called a conference to avoid war). Most of all, he was reacting to changes in relations between Austria and Russia.

What was Bismarck's priority after 1871?
Consolidation of Germany (on internal matters) required peace in Europe. He wanted to see the maintenance of the new balance of power (with Germany dominant in central Europe rather than France).

Practical assignment
Using an outline map of Europe in 1871, annotate onto to it Bismarck's diplomatic deals with each of the countries and list how these relationships changed. Try to identify from the map the inconsistencies of his policy and how the 'system', if it can be called that, broke down under Wilhelm II.

Study and revision tips
Try to become conversant with the similarities and differences of Bismarck's and Wilhelm's domestic and foreign policies. This can be done simply by listing the ways in which each social and political group was dealt with in two columns on a side of paper. Try to assess why historians dub Wilhelm's rule a 'new course'.

4

The Eastern Question

One-minute summary – The Ottoman Empire was an ancient and decaying institution. Already weakened before the mid-nineteenth century, it had lost control of North Africa and parts of the Balkans. Yet, it showed remarkable resilience and was supported by the British and then the Germans as a power that could contain Russia. Its potential collapse was the source of tension in Europe and a number of crises occurred when territories tried to break away from Constantinople's rule. In each case, the problems of the region attracted international interest and drew in the Great Powers.

In this chapter you will learn about:

▶ the problems of the Ottoman Empire
▶ the significance of the Eastern Question 1875–78
▶ the Balkan states and the Bulgarian Question 1885–86
▶ the Turkish nationalists and their aspirations.

The Ottoman Empire

The Ottoman Empire appeared to be on the verge of collapse

The Osman (translated to Ottoman) dynasty, rooted in the Turkic-speaking and Islamic region of central Asia, created an Empire that lasted from 1288 to 1922. It had once been a formidable military power that had invaded Europe, occupying part of Spain and lands as far north as Vienna. However, by 1870, most Europeans regarded the Ottoman Empire as 'the sick man of Europe'. Despite a vast territory, and some remaining military power, the Turkish-ruled Empire had fallen into decay. There were a number of reasons for this. Its civil service had become corrupt and inefficient. There was bitter rivalry between factions at the court of the supreme ruler, the Sultan. The Janissaries, an élite military force and palace guard, also wielded conservative political power. Many of the officials were Christians recruited, or enslaved, from the provinces of the Balkans, and provincial rulers (Pashas) grew increasingly independent as the nineteenth century wore on. Nationalist ideas were spreading through the Balkans and Turkey had already lost Greece (independent 1829), Serbia and Romania (autonomous 1829 and 1858 respectively), and the Ionian Islands (to Greece, 1863). The Empire faced a number of rebellions, and when this involved Greece (the home of the Orthodox Church), or the rich lands on the Danube Delta, Russia became involved. Anxious about Russian expansion and assistance the Tsar might give to fellow Slav peoples in the Balkans, the Austrian Empire rivalled the Russians in the region.

The legacy of the Crimean War was suspicion between East and West

Other powers had interests in the eastern Mediterranean. France regarded it as a Catholic duty to protect or supervise Egypt, Syria and the holy places of the Near East. More prosaically, they saw the Mediterranean as a 'French lake', the control of which was vital to the security of southern France and its trade. Great Britain also saw the Mediterranean as a vital artery of trade to the east. It regarded a Russian-controlled Balkans as a nightmare scenario, since warships would be able to interfere with British shipping at will. A severed trade route would affect Britain's prosperity. Moreover, Russian designs on central Asia seemed to threaten Britain's largest colonial possession, India. When Russia tried to occupy the mouth of the Danube in 1853, threatening Constantinople, Britain and France, allied with Turkey, fought Russia in the Crimean War (1854–56). Russia was defeated and was forced to neutralise the Black Sea (removing all warships and naval bases from its coastline). However, when France was defeated in 1871, Russia compelled Britain, by the Convention of London, to permit the remilitarisation of the Black Sea. Deep suspicion remained on both sides. The continuing instability of Turkey, and Russia's eagerness to assert itself as the defender of Balkan Christians, made further conflict likely.

The Eastern Question 1875–78

Russian intrigues were common

In the second half of the nineteenth century, Russian intellectuals justified the country's expansionist aspirations in the Balkans as Pan-Slavism. The existence of Slav languages (Russian, Serbo-Croat, Czech and Bulgarian) was thought to be based on a common Slavic heritage. In 1867, the Tsar presided over a great ethnic exhibition where he addressed all the delegates as 'brother Slavs'. In 1870, the Russians demanded, via the Bulgarians under Turkish rule, the creation of a Slavic Church supervised by the Greek Patriarch at Constantinople. On 10 March that year, the Sultan's *firman* (edict) complied, but the exarch (leader) of the new church was a Bulgar. This caused a great deal of rivalry and infighting. The case revealed both Russian and Turkish intrigue. The Russians were clearly trying to increase their influence over all the peoples of the Balkans, prior to its 'liberation' from Turkish rule. The Turks, realising the threat, deliberately set the Slavs against one another to, as Machiavelli would have put it, 'divide and rule'.

Pan-Slav agitation focused on Bulgaria but bore fruit in Bosnia

Russian and Pan-Slav agents began to stir the people of the Balkans who were still under Turkish rule with propaganda. They exploited the genuine discontent with the corrupt and inefficient rule of the Turks, and the differences of religion between themselves and their Muslim overlords. The Pan-Slav Central Committee, with offices at Moscow and Bucharest, played on racial animosity and the nationalism of the people, especially in Bulgaria (which Russia hoped to acquire). However, in 1874 the harvest in Bosnia and Herzegovina failed. Facing hardship, the peasants refused to pay taxes or perform the labour service demanded by the Turks and the landowners. They were also angry with the 'Young Turk' movement (an organisation calling for reform of the Ottoman Empire and the ruthless persecution of Christians) and despised the Turkish authorities. In 1875, rebellion broke out. Such was the international interest in the region, that immediately all the Great Powers were involved.

Attempts to stop the rebellion failed

Britain, Austria and Russia all aimed to stop the rebellion in Bosnia, but could not agree on a common policy. On 30 December 1875, the *Dreikaiserbund* powers (Austria, Germany, Russia) issued the Andrassy Note, urging Turkey to sign an armistice and implement reforms. Britain and France agreed but were disappointed not to have been consulted. The Turks appeared to ignore the Note, and their irregular troops, the Bashi-Bazouks, slaughtered 12,000 Bulgarian civilians in a reign of terror. The action caused widespread anger in Europe. In May 1876, Germany, Austria and Russia tried to enforce an armistice by issuing the Berlin Memorandum, and called for the formation of a Christian-Muslim tribunal to implement reforms. Disraeli, Britain's premier, rejected the Memorandum as it threatened military operations if the reforms were not carried out, and the Sultan had no intention of carrying out the reforms anyway. On 30 June, the Serbs and Montenegrins declared war on Turkey, but were routed. With Belgrade about to be captured, the Serbs appealed to Russia for help. The prospect of war with Russia persuaded the Sultan to end the conflict and he agreed to a conference at Constantinople that December.

The breakdown of relations between Turkey and Russia

The Ottoman Empire was heading towards bankruptcy in 1874, and international financiers had begun to take over some of the fiscal administration of Turkey. It was hoped that with greater financial stability, Sultan Abdul Hamid II would be able to make internal reforms. Disraeli was confident that this could be achieved without Russian interference. However, the Sultan continued to reject constitutional changes despite some suggestions that he might do so. Russia consulted Austria and Germany about their reactions to Russian intervention. Bismarck was unwilling to see any German troops committed to the region, saying that there were 'no German interests worth the bones of a single Pomeranian musketeer'. Austria, by the terms of the Budapest Convention (January 1877), would remain neutral in a Russo-Turkish war but would be permitted to annex Bosnia and Herzegovina (as compensation for its loss of influence over the German states), whilst Russia would get Bessarabia on the Danube (which she had lost in 1856). Both sides agreed that no large state should be established on their southern borders. In April 1877, the Tsar gave way to the Pan-Slav demands for action and war was declared.

Russia's quick victory failed to materialise

Despite the assistance of irregulars from the Balkans, the Russians under General Todleben were held up for six months by the determined defence of the fortress of Plevna. Osman Pasha's troops ruined Russian plans for a lightning strike through Bulgaria to Constantinople (which would forestall international intervention). When the breakthrough came, on 10 December, the other European powers were more sympathetic to the Turks who had defended their country against great odds. By January 1878, the Russians were at Adrianople, apparently poised to take the capital, and they had overrun the Turkish Caucasus, but suspicions of Russian intentions provoked the British and Austrians into action. A British fleet sailed to Constantinople to remind the Russians that any agreement must be an international one, whilst Austria mobilised her army and suggested a conference be held. Russia hastily concluded its own treaty, San Stefano, with Turkey on 3 March 1878. The most important provisions of this agreement were the creation of a large Bulgaria initially under Russian control, the annexation by Russia of Turkey's lands in the Caucasus, and the independence of the pro-Russian provinces of Serbia and Montenegro.

There were strong reactions to the Russian Treaty of San Stefano

In principle, the creation of an independent 'big' Bulgaria offered the chance for the Balkan peoples to resist Turkish oppression, but Austria objected to the failure to acknowledge her own designs on Bosnia, whilst Britain was concerned by the extension of Russian influence in the region. Romania was dissatisfied with the award of southern Dobruja since she had joined Russia in the war against Turkey and yet would lose the rich Bessarabia to her ally. The other Balkan provinces were also resentful of the large Bulgaria proposal which would threaten their interests. Britain's threat of war with Russia over San Stefano and Bismarck's suggestion of a conference led to the Congress of Berlin in June –July 1878. Many of the proposals were settled in advance so the Congress went smoothly. Bismarck, while appearing to be the 'honest broker' between rivals, was actually concerned to keep Austria and Russia from going to war with each other. Bismarck paid tribute to the diplomatic skills of Disraeli, remarking: 'Ach, der alte Jude, der ist der Mann' (ah, the old Jew, he is the leading man).

The Congress of Berlin preserved peace for a time in the Balkans

Austria was granted the right to administer the provinces of Bosnia-Herzegovina and the Sanjak of Novibazar, although they remained under Turkish suzerainty (a form of sovereignty). Britain received the colony of Cyprus from Turkey (as a base in the eastern Mediterranean). 'Big' Bulgaria was reduced, and it lost the province of Eastern Rumelia which remained under Turkish rule (with an approved Christian governor) even though its population was Bulgarian. Serbia, Montenegro and Romania were enlarged and became independent nation states. Romania was forced to give up Bessarabia for Dobruja. Russia, which lost its large Bulgaria, got the valuable Danubian Bessarabia. It retained its influence over the new independent Bulgaria through military advisors and political agents. Turkey finally promised further internal reform, although, once again, this failed to materialise. Whilst thousands of Balkan peoples returned to Turkish rule, it was hoped the Congress, a classic example of international co-operation and peace-making, would prove long lasting. Yet Turkey's weaknesses were more evident than ever and her north African territories were soon annexed by the Europeans (Tunisia in 1881 by France, Egypt in 1882 by Britain). Bulgarians were dissatisfied with the severing of Roumelia and future conflict seemed likely. Russia was also bitterly disappointed by the results of a difficult war and by Bismarck's apparent favouring of Austria (particularly in light of the Dual Alliance of 1879).

There was likely to be trouble in the Balkans in the future

Romania was angry at its treatment in 1878 and was likely to seek change. It allied itself to Austria, Russia's rival in 1882, which brought it into Germany's sphere too. Serbia was also dissatisfied by Russia's abandonment of her and she allied with Austria in 1881. Greece felt that, after a limited support of Russia in 1878, it should have been rewarded with Thessaly, but this province was returned to Turkey. The Greeks felt that they had a right to Macedonia and Thrace. Russia, having lost its support in the Balkans, was more reliant than ever on Bulgaria and made strenuous efforts to increase its influence there. Russia also looked to central Asia for future opportunities for expansion, which brought the Tsar into greater conflict with Britain.

The Balkan States and the Bulgarian Question 1885–86

Bulgaria grew resentful of Russian influence

Under its new constitution, the *Sobranje* (assembly) elected Alexander of Battenberg (the Tsar's nephew) to be the King of Bulgaria in April 1879. Russian officials owed their allegiance to the Tsar and they tended to treat Bulgaria as a subordinate province of Russia. Bulgarian officials looked to Alexander of Battenberg for leadership. When the Russians objected to the Bulgarian preference for Austrian support for a railway project, matters came to a head, and, in 1883, Alexander of Battenberg dismissed the Russian ministers. Whilst the dispute was still unresolved, a rebellion against Turkish rule broke out in Eastern Roumelia in September 1885. It was soon apparent that the Roumelians were demanding union with Bulgaria. Russia objected, concerned that it was losing control of Bulgaria, whilst Austria and Britain, although initially hesitant, saw an advantage in supporting an anti-Russian state. Serbia and Romania were not eager to see Bulgaria, a neighbour, enlarged. Serbia immediately attacked Bulgaria, but its forces were decisively defeated. Serbia was saved by Austrian intervention. In the spring of 1886, Roumelia and Bulgaria were united.

Figure 3. The Balkans in 1870.

Russia responded aggressively

The Tsar was furious at the loss of influence over Bulgaria and ordered Alexander of Battenberg to be kidnapped in August 1886. Stambulov, the Bulgar leader, demanded his release, which was eventually achieved. However, the king attracted suspicion on his return, as Bulgarians weren't sure if the Russians had browbeaten him into submission. He abdicated as an unpopular figure in September. Russia considered an invasion of Bulgaria to impose a new puppet ruler. This compelled Austria to begin military preparations of her own. When General Boulanger seemed poised to take power in France, many believed that a war against Germany, and therefore Austria too, would result. This was greeted with enthusiasm in Russia. In July 1887, the Bulgarians chose Ferdinand, a former Hungarian officer, as their ruler. This was further proof of Bulgaria's drift towards the Austrian sphere, but it was also becoming apparent that the rest of Europe would not accept Russian intervention. The Tsar instead persuaded the Sultan to declare the selection of Ferdinand as illegal. Stambulov was unmoved and was the effective ruler of Bulgaria. His strong government eventually aroused opposition and he was force to resign later in 1894, the year before he was assassinated.

Bismarck resolved the crisis

Bismarck knew that Germany would lose out in the event of a war between Russia and Austria, because France would probably become involved and Germany would have to choose sides between its two allies. As a solution, Bismarck proposed that the Balkans be divided into two spheres of influence, the western half under Austria, the eastern under Russia. When this failed to gain support, he took steps to strengthen the German army (January 1887), which had the added effect of neutralising the opposition he faced in the Reichstag and calming French enthusiasm for war. He also renewed the alliance terms with Austria and Italy (February 1887), and signed the Reinsurance Treaty with Russia (June 1887) to prevent any combination with France. Bismarck marked with approval the British, Italian, Austrian and Spanish commitment to maintain the *status quo* in the Mediterranean, a clear sign to France, and also to Russia, that they would not accept aggression. Bismarck also refused to take Russian securities for loans, thus hampering the rouble and making it more inconvenient for Russia to wage war in the Balkans. Bismarck then published the terms of the Dual Alliance: this reminded Austria that Germany would only help if Austria was attacked, and showed the Russians that if it attacked Austria, Germany would be forced to come in on the Austrian side. In 1888, Bismarck threatened the Russians in a Reichstag speech: 'We Germans fear God, and *nothing else* in the world', implying a war with Russia held no fear for Germany.

Unrest continued in the Ottoman domains

The Turks failure to carry out any widespread political or social reforms made further unrest inevitable, and this coincided with new waves of nationalism in the new Balkan states. The Greeks, for example, wanted to gain control of Macedonia and Crete. In 1894, a patriotic secret society called *Ethnike Hetaireia* (National Society) was formed to liberate these areas. In 1896, riots broke out between Muslims and the Christian Greeks on Crete and the Greeks declared unification with their nation state on the mainland. The Greek government sent naval support and despatched troops to Thessaly. However, by 1897, the Turks had defeated the rebellion and routed Greek forces, forcing them to pay a war indemnity. A joint Anglo-French force was sent to Crete to end the fighting, but the murder of the British consul persuaded the British to expel the Turks altogether. With international approval, Prince George was selected to become the ruler of Crete which was still nominally a Turkish possession, but in fact was run as an independent island. Yet the most serious problems occurred in Armenia. In 1894 serious unrest was crushed by a series of Turkish massacres of the Gregorian Christian population. Despite Armenian appeals for assistance, Russia,

Figure 4. The Ottoman Empire in 1870.

the most likely champion stood by, eager not to repeat the error of 'ungrateful Bulgaria'. Germany, backed by Austria, took no action to win Turkish favour.

Austria and Russia began to co-operate over the Balkans

Both Russia and Austria had learned that the Balkans were dangerous if peace was to be preserved between them. In 1897 they agreed to maintain peace in the region and this was formalised by the Murzsteg Agreement of 1903. In Macedonia, which was claimed by several countries and filled with a mixture of races, Austria and Russia agreed on joint control. They established a gendarmerie, raised taxes and were charged with making reforms. Austria reneged on this agreement when Turkey offered railway construction concessions to prevent change.

The rise of the Turkish nationalists

Whilst Britain and the Mediterranean powers wanted to maintain the *status quo* in the Ottoman Empire, the Kaiser of Germany saw the opportunity for greater world influence by befriending the Turks. He made much of this 'friendship' in a tour of the Holy Lands in 1898, hoping to appear as the champion of Muslims all over the world. The German army had begun advising the Turkish forces as early as 1881, but commercial relations were also strengthened. In 1899, the Germans backed a project that would link Berlin with Baghdad by rail. Mining concessions were also granted, bankers, traders and financiers poured into Turkey. The effect of this was to persuade some Turks that their country must modernise or become a colony of Germany. They had their own ambitions about the regeneration and expansion of a Turkish empire across the Middle East. A group calling itself the 'Young Turks', or the Committee of Union and Progress, carried out a palace *coup* on 23 July 1908. Eager to reassert Turkish control over Macedonia, the reformers forced the Sultan to agree to elections for a national assembly. When the Sultan tried to rescind on these concessions, he was deposed in 1909. The new Sultan did not carry out reforms, but endorsed a policy of Turkification. Russia and Austria were concerned at this revival of the Turks, and so were the smaller Balkan states.

Serbia turned away from Austria

In 1903, the Serbian king, who had enjoyed close relations with Austria, was murdered. The Obrenovich dynasty was replaced by the rival Karageorgovich line. The new king, Peter I, was pro-Russian and supported an expansion line. He looked to the liberation of Serbs living under Austrian influence in Bosnia and Herzegovina. Austria would clearly object to the creation of larger, more powerful state on its southern border. Serbia advocated closer commercial ties with Bulgaria in 1904 in an effort to break away from Austrian influence. In 1906, the Hungarians persuade their imperial Austrian partners not to accept cheap Serbian agricultural produce and a trade war, called the 'pig war', began and lasted until 1908. The Serbians looked to Turkey and Germany as outlets for its goods. In addition loans were raised in Paris rather than in Austria, to free themselves from the influence of Vienna. The new Austrian Foreign Minister of 1906, Aerenthal, believed that Serbia must be suppressed as a threat to the Empire. He began to consider how Bulgaria might assist in the dismemberment of Serbia.

Conclusion: a period of transition

By 1908, the Ottoman Empire was undergoing rapid change. It had lost control of the Balkans and its North African possessions. It had lost influence in the Middle East too. Internally it was still in need of urgent reform, but a new aggressive nationalism in Turkey was taking over. The string of humiliations throughout the last quarter of the nineteenth century had provoked a new generation to reject the traditional methods of Ottoman rule. Turkey had also acquired new allies. Where once it had been championed by France and Britain, now Germany and Austria stood as its staunchest supporters. Russia had believed it was the natural successor of Turkish rule in the Balkans but it had been thwarted time and again. Had the Europeans been united, the Ottoman Empire may have been broken up long before, but it had, in fact, served their purpose to preserve it, or at least the rump of it. German influence ran through Turkey by 1908, and its armed forces were practically run by the German officer Liman von Sanders. However, the aggressive aspirations of Serbia and the ambitions of Austria were to be the seat of future conflict, which ultimately led to the outbreak of the First World War.

Tutorial

Progress questions
1. Why were there rebellions in the Balkans in 1875?

2. How influential were nationalism and Pan-Slavism in the events in the Balkans in this period?

3. Why were the San Stefano and Berlin Congress agreements ultimately unsatisfactory?

4. How effective was international co-operation in the Balkans, and Bismarck's diplomacy, between 1877–1890?

Discussion points
1. How far was Russia responsible for the crises in the Balkans in this period?

2. Consider a series of counterfactuals (what if...?) to understand the decision-making processes involved, such as: what if Russia had won the war of 1877 within a couple of weeks and successfully imposed San Stefano? What if the Congress of Berlin had been indecisive?

Practical assignment
This region, more than any other, requires careful scrutiny of a map to understand its history. Make a sketch map to show the ethnic distribution of the region, the territorial changes between 1878 and 1908 and annotate on the key agreements that were concluded.

Study and revision tips
This is a complex area. Concentrate on the Great Powers' actions and the general aspirations of the Balkan states to get an understanding of the period and the region.

5

The Austro-Hungarian Empire

One-minute summary – The Austro-Hungarian Empire was formed when the old Austrian Habsburg dynasty was defeated by Prussia in a short war in 1866. The Compromise of 1867 set up power sharing between the Austrians and the Hungarians, in two quite distinct halves of the empire. However, the failure to accommodate the other national minorities caused considerable unrest. Tension continued between the Austrian and Hungarian authorities, which developed into a constitutional crisis in 1905. Faced by economic problems and internal unrest, the Empire then found itself confronted by external challenges from newly independent Slavic states like Serbia. Amongst the Great Powers, Austria could generally rely on German support but Russia was a rival for Austrian influence over the economic potential of the Balkans.

In this chapter you will learn:

▶ how Austria-Hungary functioned as a dual monarchy
▶ the effect of nationalism on the empire
▶ the significance of the Balkan rivalries
▶ how historical controversies have developed around the subject.

The dual monarchy

The Habsburg monarchy was the unifying link in an Empire of many races and nationalities. Although Europe was everywhere experiencing the rise of the nation state, Austria's empire remained a medieval anachronism. Metternich, one of its leading chancellors in the early nineteenth century, confessed that he had 'given his life to propping up a mouldering edifice'. In 1815, the empire had a population of 30 million and it was recognised as one of the Great Powers of Europe. Yet the leadership of the Empire was chiefly in the hands of the German-speaking Austrians who made up 23 per cent of the people. The next largest group were the Magyars of Hungary (20 per cent), then the Czechs of Bohemia and Moravia (12 per cent), the Poles and Ruthenes of Galicia (10 per cent), the Romanians of Transylvania, the Serbs, Slovenes and Croats of Dalmatia and Illystria, and, until 1866, Italians in Lombardy and Venetia. The Magyars had succeeded in gaining a number of concessions from the Austrians. They had a Diet (assembly) from 1791 but this was removed after revolutionary unrest in 1848–49. Hungarians continued to agitate for change, but when Austria was defeated by Prussia in 1866, the Hungarian leader Francis Deak refused to exploit Austria's weakness or bid for independence. Instead, in 1867, he suggested a partnership called the *Ausgleich*. Austria and Hungary were to be independent but linked by common interests.

Figure 5. The Austro-Hungrian Empire in 1870.

The form of the Austro-Hungarian Empire was a partnership

Franz Josef remained the ruler of the Empire, he was crowned King of Hungary but called Emperor elsewhere. Joint ministries continued to run military and foreign affairs. The imperial assembly met alternately in Vienna and Budapest. Annual delegations met to decide matters of common interest, a decennial treaty was set up to regulate tariffs, currency, and military matters. Austria remained dominant in authority over the various nationalities, although they could now use their own language in state matters. The Magyars now enjoyed the same kind of authority as the Austrians over subject races in their sphere, particularly the southern Slavs and the Romanians of Transylvania. The Czechs also agitated for equal status in 1871 but Franz Josef was dissuaded from making any concessions, lest it lead to similar demands from other peoples. As a result, the Czechs boycotted the imperial and provincial parliaments until 1878. Thus, while incorporating the aspirations of the Hungarians temporarily strengthened the Empire, the Austrian régime looked less secure when one remembers it had been forced into this position. Moreover, the ruthless Magyarisation of the southern Slavs, or suppression of the Czechs, merely fuelled further nationalist unrest. So, while language concessions were granted to the Croats in 1868, in 1874 the Magyars concentrated the vote into their own hands, Slovak cultural organisations were dissolved and the number of Slovak schools was reduced (from 2,000 in

1868 to 241 in 1905).

The conservatives used the nationalities issue to their advantage

Franz Josef had been forced to accept the loss of absolute power by the 1867 Compromise. The judiciary were made independent and ministers were responsible to the imperial assembly. However, having accepted these changes, and having given some consideration to the Czech issue, he became fixed in his determination to make no further amendments. The state bureaucracy, which had always slowed changes, was to be utilised for conservatism. Moreover, with the liberals dominant in the Austrian assembly (passing reforms of court procedures, abolishing church control of schools and establishing elementary education), the élites decided to make use of the nationalities' aspirations to balance the power of the liberals. The 1879 Premier, Count Edward Taffe, invited the Czechs to form a coalition with the conservatives and the church, called the 'Iron Ring'. In return, Taffe granted the Czechs a chance to gain the majority of the Bohemian Diet under a new electoral law (1882) and of the Bohemian section of the Reichsrat (upper house of the imperial assembly). The university of Prague was divided into a German and a Czech section, and Czech was permitted as an official language of the state. The Poles were also encouraged to join the Iron Ring and were granted similar concessions in Galicia against the Ruthenes. Taffe survived longer than any previous minister because of this ability to weld different groups together but he also enjoyed the confidence of the Emperor.

Nationalism

Austrian German nationalist movements felt humiliated

After Taffe's ministry ended in 1893, new, more extremist politics developed in the empire. A Pan-German movement emerged, as did an organisation calling itself the Young Czechs. Slavs looked to their own Pan-Slavic movement. The German element was angry at the loss of the traditional German domination of the Empire. In contrast to the vigorous new Germany to the north, the régime in Vienna seemed moribund, and, under Taffe, too eager to appease the foreign minorities. Georg von Schonerer argued that German Austrians were racially superior, and in 1898 he urged the German army to invade in order to liberate the Germans in Austria. He was also a committed enemy of Jews. The Pan-Germans organised demonstrations and there was serious rioting in Prague in 1893 and again in 1897. Karl Lueger, by contrast, was mayor of Vienna (1897–1907) and he led a Christian Socialist Party which combined Catholicism, anti-capitalism and anti-Semitism. He was supported by the artisans and shopkeepers who distrusted the Jews and big business, and who approved of his programme of municipal socialism. An early adherent of this organisation was the young Adolf Hitler.

The Emperor reluctantly introduced universal suffrage

On the left, the Austrian Social Democratic Party was boosted by the introduction of universal manhood suffrage in 1907. There had been general agreement between all parties on the need to extend the franchise and reforms had begun in 1897. In 1901, concessions were extended to the Czechs. A period of unrest and heated debate followed where it was almost impossible to conduct parliamentary business. The Emperor dissolved the *Reichstag*, but the unrest worsened. Thus universal suffrage was granted to all men over 24 and foreign minorities were given a proportionate degree of representation. The SPD won 87 seats in the election of the new *Reichstag* and was strongly represented in the cities. The Party was revolutionary in theory, but like the German SPD, it was reformist or gradualist in practice.

The stability of the Empire was in doubt

There were still considerable strengths in the Empire despite the disturbances at the turn of the century. The agricultural regions of Hungary and the east supplied the more industrial and urbanised western provinces. The forces of the right, the church, the élites, the army and the bureaucracy, were all united and enjoyed an alliance with the foreign minorities. However, further concessions to these groups seemed unlikely, as it would antagonise their Hungarian partners. The Hungarians were always concerned to strengthen their own position over minorities in their sphere and they did not wish to see any precedent of concessions being set by the Austrians. There was still tension between the Hungarians and Austrians over tariffs. Both sides wanted to retain protectionism, but the Hungarians obtained favourable advantages in their agricultural produce, whilst refusing to accept any changes to the tariffs on imported Austrian manufactures. Hungary contributed less than a third of all the military costs of the Empire which angered the Austrians, yet the Magyars also sought a separate army and control over their own foreign affairs. In effect this would have meant a complete severance of the old ties.

Hungarian nationalism was the chief threat to the Empire

The Hungarians, or rather the small land-owning strata of Magyar society that held power, retained restrictions on the franchise in 1874 thus allowing only 800,000 to participate in elections. Ninety-five per cent of all officials were Magyars as well as ninety per cent of all the judges. Eighty per cent of all the newspapers were in Magyar. Schools, businesses, the legal system and the police force were all subject to the language restriction. Only the Croats had a modicum of autonomy in their own Diet. Kalman Tisza, the premier between 1875 and 1890, centralised the communications infrastructure during a period of relative prosperity, but the onset of the depression in the 1890s gave rise to new, more nationalist organisations like the National Party, led by Albert Apponyi and the Independence Party led by Ferenc Kossuth, son of the Hungarian nationalist hero of 1849. There was greater enthusiasm for Hungarian independence and a cultural renaissance of its nationalist achievements. However, the Emperor opposed any demands for the use of Hungarian as the language of the army, believing it would cause confusion and weaken the forces. He dissolved the House of Deputies with troops and threatened to close Austrian markets to Hungarian grain and, more importantly, impose universal suffrage, knowing this would end the Magyar domination of the assembly, or at least the rule of the Hungarian oligarchy. The threat worked and the Magyars' demands were withdrawn but there was no solution to Magyarisation. Croats lost their constitution in 1912 and unrest amongst the minorities prompted a general strike that same year.

Balkan rivalries

Austria-Hungary's fate was closely tied to events in the Balkans. In 1902, the Magyars, using the Serbs as their supporters, had forcibly suppressed the Croats. However, the change of régime in Belgrade opened a new anti-Austro-Hungarian chapter in Serbia. Meanwhile, in Transylvania, Magyar suppression of an independence movement caused anger in neighbouring Romania. The Hungarians began to believe that southern Slav agitation from outside the Empire needed to be dealt with aggressively, if the Hungarians were to retain their hegemony. In this sense, the desire to dominate the Balkans fitted in with existing Austrian ambitions to create an economic sphere in the region. Andrassy, the Foreign Minister, had encouraged the development of a railway link to the Aegean (a fact which also coincided with German plans for a railway to Turkey). For the same reason, the Austrians and Hungarians wanted to retain control or influence over the strategically valuable Adriatic coast and the mouth of the Danube, one of Europe's most important river trade arteries. The change of relationship with Serbia after 1903, from cordiality to trade wars and hostility, made the Austrians recall previous problems with the Italians in the 1850s and 1860s. Serbia was called the 'Piedmont of the southern Slavs'. All hopes that the Slavs might be incorporated as the third element of the Empire, along with the Austrians and Magyars, (a view promoted by the so-called 'Trialists') was abandoned. The annexation of Bosnia in 1908 opened a new, more bitter phase in the Balkans and put Serbia and the Austro-Hungarian Empire on a collision course.

Historical controversies

Most histories of the Austro-Hungarian Empire have focused on why it lasted so long. The key questions are: was it doomed to collapse after the 1867 Compromise, or was it only really destroyed by the First World War? To the 'inevitable' school belonged Oscar Jaszi who argued in 1929 that the exclusion of the Slavs from participation in the regime created an insurmountable degree of domestic opposition. Edward Crankshaw and Hugo Hantsch took a different view. They argued that whilst the nationalists were important, it was a reform of the existing régime they wanted, not the abolition of the Empire. In their analysis, the war destroyed the old Empire. John Mason, in *The Dissolution of the Austro-Hungarian Empire* (1985) argued that a synthesis of these two viewpoints is necessary. A.J.P. Taylor stressed that the 1866 defeat of Austria was a disaster because, not only did it force the Austrians to make concessions and thus inspire the Slav nationalities to demand more compromises, but it also made Austria more dependent on German leadership in their foreign policy.

A final verdict?

Taylor was only right up to a point: in the events leading to the Great War, it was Austria that drew Germany into a conflict, not the other way around. It was, in fact, Austria's inability to solve the Balkans problem, which, coupled with its own internal crisis (itself mainly generated by the Hungarians rather than the Austrians), compelled her to seek more radical solutions. The irony was that the Serb terrorists, who assassinated Franz Ferdinand, the heir to the Austrian throne, on 28 June 1914, killed the one man who may have begun the process of inclusion of Slavs in the Empire on a more equal footing to balance Hungarian power. Yet the war should have been a localised Balkan conflict. The fact that it was not, and that it was already a precedent that the Great Powers would be involved, can only be understood in relation to the wider issues of the Eastern question and power politics.

Tutorial

Progress questions

1. What were the unifying influences of the Austro-Hungarian Empire?

2. How did the conservative élites of Austria use the nationality issue to their advantage?

3. Why was Magyarisation a threat to the future of the Empire?

Discussion point

Why did the *Ausgleich* create as many problems as it solved?

Practical assignment

Once again, the use of a map is vital in this subject. Try to locate the various national groups in the Austro-Hungarian Empire. Note its geographical position *vis-à-vis* the other Great Powers, and the distribution of the major mountain ranges and rivers which affected its economy. Compare the economic performance of the Empire with Germany and Russia. On a sketch map, try to annotate on the aspirations of each of the national groups. What arguments did they use to justify inclusion in the political decision-making of the Empire?

Study and revision tips

1. The chief questions of how the Empire survived are favoured by examiners. Consider how you could argue all sides effectively. Look at the evidence of the Empire's weakness, but also try to list the factors that held it together so effectively.

2. Concentrate on the relations between the German-speaking Austrians and the Magyars. Note how the Slav question was as much an external matter as an internal one. For more help, consult the main headings in Chapter 4.

3. There are several similarities in the problems the Empire faced with the Russian Empire. A comparative exercise can help you to understand the issues involved.

6

Russia, 1870–1914

One-minute summary – When Russia began to dismantle the old feudal system of land ownership, there was wide expectation that Russia was moving to a more democratic future. Yet the reforms were designed to strengthen, not weaken, the autocracy of the Tsars. Since the people had no representation except the regional councils and village communes, frustration led to the emergence of revolutionary organisations. The régime tried to carry out economic reforms, but feared the consequences of industrialisation. In essence, the Tsars were faced with one insurmountable contradiction. They wanted to retain all the powers and privileges of the medieval autocrats, but they wanted to create a modern, industrialised economy. In the event, the rulers turned to repression and nationalism, and every episode of unrest made them more determined to retain control. The solutions they proposed were 'too little, too late' and a fatalistic resignation began to set in the years before the war.

In this chapter you will learn:

▶ how the Tsarist régime functioned
▶ why there were revolutionary organisations and the state policy of reaction
▶ what economic problems Russia faced and how they were dealt with
▶ what condition Russia was in on the eve of the revolutions
▶ how Russia conducted its foreign policy
▶ the historical controversies that have surrounded this subject.

The Tsarist régime

Russia's scale was both a strength and a weakness
Russia's size, occupying one-sixth of the world's land surface in 1815, gave the country a 'Great Power' status. The population, standing at 97.7 million in 1880, provided the manpower for agriculture, industry and the armed forces on a massive scale. However, Russia's size was also a disadvantage. Its land frontiers ran for thousands of miles, huge belts of its territory was totally unproductive and its infrastructure was stretched between its dispersed population centres. In the Crimean War (1854–56), it had proved difficult to reinforce and supply its troops even within its own national borders.

The structure of society reflected the Tsar's powerful position
The Tsar was an autocrat with considerable powers. He was able to make laws at will and was the supreme head of state. The Tsar's court consisted of ministers and

Figure 6. The Russia Empire in 1870.

civil servants, and promotion was often dependent on favouritism. The administrators made up about 3.7 per cent of the population. The clergy of the Orthodox Church, led by the Patriarch in St Petersburg, supported the régime by preaching deference and obedience. The army was a vast and loyal institution, making up 5 per cent of the population. Reforms after the Crimean War by Dimitri Milyutin had improved terms of service, but it was still an organisation that demanded obedience to authority. Much of the Russian army was deployed on internal security duties, and was sometimes used to crush rebellion or break strikes. The noblemen, the titled aristocracy, had strong links with the army and the church, and they could be relied upon to support the régime. The industrial workers were a small group concentrated in the larger towns and cities, but they were subjected to harsh working conditions and had few rights. The peasants were the largest group in society (83 per cent in the early nineteenth century), who, although freed from a system of serfdom, remained impoverished.

The Edict of Emancipation freed the serfs

The system of serfdom had been abolished by Alexander II by the Edict of Emancipation in 1861. Serfs had been 'tied' to the land to provide service to landowners or to the state. Private landowners could require a serf to work three days a week on his estate (the *Barschina*) or pay a rent (*Obrok*) for exemption. The landlord delegated the day-to-day management of a serf's affairs, and the distribution of land to the village commune (the *Mir*) which was dominated by the elders. Serfs could be bought or sold, their land expropriated, marriages arranged and the law administered over them without representation. The status of a nobleman depended on the number of 'souls' he owned. State serfs had been liable to conscription, but capital punishment was not permitted. The Edict (*Ukase*) of 1861 had been conceived as early as 1855, but Nikolai Milyutin, the 'enlightened bureaucrat' Deputy Minister of the Interior, was cautious, taking several years to consult with the noblemen of the provinces. Twenty-one million serfs were freed along with twenty million 'state peasants'. Peasants received the land they had worked and noblemen were compensated with government bonds. However, the consequences of the abolition of serfdom reverberated throughout the rest of the nineteenth century.

The Edict had drawbacks and was insincere

The government aimed to recoup its expenditure on bonds by compelling the peasants to pay Redemption Dues. They had to pay 20–25 per cent of the purchase price and pay for the rest at 6 per cent interest over 49 years. The *Mir* held the land collectively until the payments were complete, which, along with the assumption of the landlord's former responsibilities, greatly empowered the village elders. Alexander was heralded as the 'Tsar Liberator'. Hugh Seton-Watson regarded the emancipation as more successful, more significant and less violent than the freeing of black slaves in America in the same period. However, the reform may not have been as sincere as it first appears. Debts amongst the nobility had forced them to drive the serfs harder, resulting in an upsurge of violence. The lack of modernisation meant that production was failing to keep pace with the rising population. It was hoped that private ownership would encourage improvements to be made, and surpluses would provide funds for reinvestment and stimulate consumer demand. Nevertheless, Alexander remarked in 1856 that 'it is better to abolish serfdom from above rather than await the time when it will abolish itself from below' suggesting that emancipation was driven by a desire to avoid rebellion and disorder.

The results of emancipation were not as positive as expected

Many peasants feared change, and were particularly angry that they had to pay the Redemption Dues for land that they had farmed for years and which they felt they truly owned. Some peasants received less land than they expected, and the average landholding was just nine acres. This would promote intensive farming, but only half of the peasants were able to produce a surplus. Former 'privately owned' serfs received no land and had to serve a further two years after the *Ukase*, but received wages in return. The Redemption payments were often high because landowners exaggerated the value of their holdings, but this meant that, in order to pay the Dues, the peasants had to return to work for their former masters or rent half their land to the landowner and pay for the rents with crops. Some peasants began to buy up plots from others. The peasants who 'sold up' drifted into the towns looking for work. The terms of the Edict were not always implemented straight away and it was not until 1881 that the transfer of lands was finally made compulsory. The indebtedness of the landowners meant that much of the compensation was absorbed in wiping out debts and little money was invested in agricultural modernisation. Landowners remained in debt so that, by 1905, a third of their land was sold and 50 per cent was mortgaged.

The village communes were empowered

The *Mir* was responsible for the taxation of the whole community and it could control almost every aspect of its agriculture. The effect was to stifle the more entrepreneurial farmers. Peasants could not leave the land until payments for their land had been delivered, and any travel had to be authorised by the *Mir*. The net result of the indebtedness and restrictions of the *Mir* was the continued stagnation of Russian farming. However, it is important to take a balanced viewpoint. New labour was released for industrialisation. The emancipation passed relatively peacefully (there were 647 riots in the four months after the Edict), and the abolition of serfdom brought a degree of modernisation to Russia.

Alexander also reformed local government in 1864

It followed that with the abolition of serfdom, the political structure, which had relied on a system of deference and ownership, would also need to be updated. The landowners were replaced as the provincial authorities by the *zemstva*. These local councils were responsible for education, health, poor relief, road construction, public services and economic development. Each district *zemstvo*, consisting of 45 per cent noblemen, 40 per cent peasantry and 15 per cent townsfolk and clergy, elected the representatives for the higher level provincial *zemstvo*. In 1870, the towns were able to set up local councils (the *duma*) through elections (males over 25). There was no control over the army or police which were controlled by the central government. Political discussions were also banned and the *zemstva* were restricted in 1865–67 when it was decreed that noblemen should make up 75 per cent of their numbers. However, the *zemstva* provided a useful training ground for those who sought political experience.

Legal reforms also took place in 1864

As noblemen no longer administered justice over their serfs, the legal system was changed. The *zemstva* nominated justices of the peace for three-year terms. The secretive nature of trials was abolished with cases being heard in public. Juries and appeal courts were set up. Lawyers' salaries were raised to prevent bribery. Whilst martial law could still be imposed, Seton-Watson believed the courts were the one place where freedom of speech truly existed. Once again, the legal system provided training for those with political aspirations.

Reforms of the armed forces improved conditions

It was said that before the reforms, families whose sons had been selected for military service would hold a virtual funeral for the departing recruit, so convinced were they that he would never return. The length of military service had already been reduced from 25 to 16 years, but, without any leave, army life was more like a prison sentence. Six-year terms of enlistment were thus introduced, and the use of the army as a place for punishing criminals was abolished. Military colonies (where sons of soldiers were sent as the recruits of the future) were abolished too and conditions in barracks improved. Basic education was made available. In 1874, the introduction of universal military service ended the exemption privileges of the middle and upper classes.

Reforms in education were a step in the process of liberalisation

A.S. Norov, the Minister of Education, abolished most of the repressive measures in Russian education. The number of university students was allowed to increase (1855), lectures on European government (1857) and philosophy (1860) were legalised. Universities were also given greater autonomy. These measures indicated the desire of the government to liberalise education, but the motive was also to produce the sort of educated classes that could emulate the West and replicate its mid-nineteenth century economic success.

The onset of reaction: the Polish Revolt was a nationalist struggle

Poland enjoyed a special status in the Russian Empire. In the late eighteenth century, Poland had been a powerful independent nation state, but in the 1790s, Poland had been carved up by Prussia, Austria and Russia. After the Congress of Vienna (1815), the Great Powers had determined that Poland should remain under Russian rule but be given a degree of autonomy. The Tsar was the King of Poland, and the country had a constitution, a parliament and used its own language in the business of government. A rebellion in 1830 had caused some of the Polish privileges to be eroded, but Alexander II had permitted the restoration of the Catholic archbishopric of Warsaw (1856) and established a new Agricultural Society (1857) to improve farming. The Society became the focus of land reform but also of nationalist aspirations and, in 1861, Alexander dissolved it. In the demonstrations that followed, 200 were killed. The Viceroy, Constantine (the Tsar's brother) was almost assassinated. Concessions were offered in the form of the emancipation of Jews and the opening of a university in Warsaw, but the idea that Poles would be conscripted into the Russian army merely fuelled a full-blown revolt in January 1863.

The revolt was crushed but Alexander's policy changed

The rebellion was concentrated in the countryside but not all the landowners sided with the peasant rebels. It was not suppressed until August 1864. As a concession, land reform was carried out and 700,000 peasants were given freehold tenure of their land without any redemption payments. This was a liberal gesture, but Hugh Seton-Watson argued that this was simply a move to divide the Polish peasants from their landowners. Alexander believed the ingratitude of Poland was symptomatic of the rest of Russia and he was disillusioned, but in fact the rebellion was just as much the result of Polish frustration with Russian authoritarian rule. Alexander was persuaded that the only future policy towards foreign minorities should be one of Russification.

Repression returned

It was not just the Polish Revolt that changed Alexander's mind about his reforms. An assassination attempt in 1866 by a fanatic called Karakosov also focused his attention on revolutionary opposition. The land reforms had taken years of planning, ostensibly to avoid rebellions, but had they gone too far? Essentially, Alexander was trying to modernise and yet retain the ancient institutions of power; it was case of changing to stay the same. Certainly the right-wing élites in Russia took exception to Alexander's reforms. This is evident when one considers the steps he took. Censorship of the press was reimposed, and the educational concessions were modified. The government took over the universities again and science was dropped from the syllabus to prevent the spread of atheism. In 1868, the *zemstva* lost their powers of taxation and they were supervised by Tsarist agents. In 1878, a woman called Vera Zasulich tried to murder the Prefect of Police, Trepov, and when she was acquitted it was decreed that she and all other political criminals were to be transferred to a courts martial without a jury.

Revolutionary organisations and reaction

There was considerable opposition to the régime which Alexander had not expected. In many ways, this was not so much dissatisfaction with the reforms but expectations about the future. The peasants, for example, felt the emancipation would be the beginning of greater social and economic freedom, but the inadequacy of the reforms and the absence of any further change in their favour caused resentment. The liberal and intellectual groups of Russia expected to see the formation of a *duma*, but the Tsar insisted on maintaining autocracy. The greater freedoms of the early 1860s also encouraged committed opponents of Tsarism to speak out more boldly. A very Russian form of opposition was the Populists movement (*narodniki*) which was formed in 1869 and led by Nikolai Mikhailovsky and Pyotr Lavrov. Their aim was to solve the land issue in favour of the peasants and encourage the village commune as the means to advance to socialism, without the need to endure the industrial revolution and its miseries which they could see in the West. They dressed as peasants in a campaign called 'to the people' in 1874, touring the countryside to agitate for reform. Three thousand young activists were met by a disbelieving peasant population. The police, who had been tipped off by the peasants themselves, rounded up 1,600 of the *narodniki*. Undeterred, Mikhail Bakunin, Lavrov and Nikolai Chernyshevsky formed a new group called *Zemlya i Volya* ('Land and Liberty') in 1876, which set out to live amongst the peasants for long periods, getting to know their ways and their beliefs. The first trade unions were also formed by Land and Liberty members in Odessa (1875) and St Petersburg (1878), but the government hunted down the members.

There were a number of opposition thinkers in Russia advocating peaceful change

Russian opposition to Tsarism took two forms in this period. There were those who preferred a gradualist path of change, rejecting, where possible, the travails of the industrialisation of the West, and there were those who wanted violent and abrupt change. The lack of progress in social justice in Russia tended to make revolutionary groups more and more radical. Terrorism had become widespread by 1914. An example of the early intellectual moderation can be found in the work of V. Belinsky, who advocated social literature versus oppression. This was followed by Alexander Herzen, who published the *Kolokol* in exile in London and advocated self-governing communes: it was he who founded populism. But Herzen applauded the reforms of the régime, an idea that did not carry favour with Chernyshevsky whose novel *What Is To Be Done?* (1862) suggested a fundamental change in Russia's social and economic base as the only means for progression. Chernyshevsky disagreed with those who claimed to be his disciples but who advocated violence. D.I. Pisarev called on the people to accept no principle, including Tsarist rule, without question. He wanted to see a radical change in Russia's philosophical outlook, especially its moral and material basis. This prompted the novelist Turgenev to label Pisarev a nihilist: the anarchist flavour of this name appealed to Pisarev.

There were opposition groups prepared to use violence

Until 1869, when the movement collapsed and was exposed, the terrorist cell of Sergei Nechayev was the only example of a ruthless and violent organisation. The murder of one of their own activists brought Nechayev into the open. It was not until 1879, when Land and Liberty split, that a new wave of highly organised terrorism began. Georgi Plekhanov, a Marxist, and P. B. Axelrod formed a group called 'Black Partition' (*Chorny Peredyel*) which continued to advocate change through the peasants. The 'People's Will' (*Narodnaya Volya*) thought that terrorism and violence would act as the trigger for a full-scale revolution. They concentrated on assassinations, trying to focus on the Tsar himself. There was an attempt to shoot him (April 1879), they tried to blow up his train (and got the wrong one) and a bomb was detonated at the Winter Palace in 1880. The other key development on the revolutionary left was initiated by Mikhail Bakunin, a member of the First International (1869) and a Marxist. At this early stage, Marxist ideas were not yet widespread and Bakunin argued with Marx over the methods and philosophy of revolution. He subsequently became an anarchist. All the revolutionaries shared a desire to see fundamental and rapid change (not gradualism) in Russia through the *narod* (people). Yet achieving this amongst a population dedicated to the Tsar seemed remote.

The revolutionaries did not succeed despite the assassination of Alexander II (1881)

Despite the growth of terrorism, Alexander appeared to be moving once again in a liberal direction when he appointed General Mikhail Loris-Melikov (the man who had captured Kars from the Turks and saved national honour in 1878) to solve unrest. Loris-Melikov was appointed Minister of the Interior in August 1880. He released hundreds of political prisoners, commuted the death sentence in many cases and urged the Tsar to consider some power sharing. On 31 March, the Tsar agreed to call a committee that would discuss the reforms. The main proposal was to have the *zemstva* co-operate with the Council of State in deciding on a new constitution. However, before the meeting convened, Alexander was killed the same day when a bomb blew off his legs. Yet, the tsarist régime did not collapse when Alexander was assassinated. Since the revolutionaries offered no realistic alternatives, and enjoyed no mass support, the old system continued.

Tsar Alexander III implemented severe repression

Inevitably after the murder, the new Tsar cracked down on revolutionary groups, but there was a reactionary policy across many aspects of Russian life. This was pre-planned. Alexander III's tutor was Constantine Pobyedonostsev, a reactionary Pan-Slav and senior official in the Russian Orthodox Church. Loris-Melikov was dismissed in favour of Pobyedonostsev. As a member of the Orthodox Church, Pobyedonostsev was convinced that other religious groups and foreign minorities needed to be crushed. Ordinary Russians often resented Jews and Pobyedonostsev encouraged anti-Semitic riots (*pogroms*). In 1891, thousands of Jews were evicted from Moscow and herded into ghettos. This served to fuel nationalistic feelings in some people and thus distract them from discontent with the régime. Minorities became scapegoats. The property of the Catholic Polish Church was confiscated (1864) and Warsaw University was closed (1869). Catholics or Poles were banned from government posts, as were the peoples of the Baltic States, the Finns, Ukrainians and Armenians. Finland's liberal constitution was undermined. Estonia and Livonia had their local liberties suspended. A tough policy of Russification was embarked upon amongst the 40 million non-Russians in the Empire, including the imposition of the Russian language in all schools. Pobyedonostsev condemned the free press and regarded democracy as 'a fatal error'.

Repressive measures were also imposed in law, local government and education

Pan-Slavism and the desire to re-establish the nobility as the foundation of the régime informed the reactionary policies of Alexander III's government. In July 1889, the position of Justice of the Peace was abolished in favour of a new post: *Zemsky Nachalnik* (Land Commandant). The post holder had to be of noble birth and had jurisdiction over all local government including the *zemstva*. Laws of 1890 and 1892 revised the franchise of the *zemstva*, restricting the popular vote. Certain issues could not be discussed, such as government policy. This was used as an excuse to block and veto almost every proposal of the *zemstva*. R. Charques remarked that this measure: 'brought back the breath and being of serf law'. The universities were subject to the revisions of the Minister of Education, I.V. Delyanov. He reduced the autonomy of these institutions (1884) and raised tuition fees (1887). Even in elementary and secondary education, new fees were designed to keep the poorer paid in their place. Parish elementary schools, under the close control of the clergy, were permitted a degree of autonomy. Whilst the educated and wealthy élite continued to produce some of the century's finest cultural works (Chekov, Tolstoy, Tchaikovsky), in 1897 79 per cent of Russia's population remained illiterate.

The accession of Nicholas II did not change the repressive policies

Despite some hope that the death of Alexander III in 1894 (through insomnia and migraines) might bring a new liberal phase in the régime, there was bitter disappointment when Nicholas II continued the old policies. In 1903, Finland's constitution was abolished, in direct contravention of the original agreement of 1815 which had established Russian rule there. Russification was also intensified. Most of the students at the university of Yuriev (formerly Dorpat) at Riga were Russian. Anti-Jewish *pogroms* continued, with 215 outbreaks between 1881 and 1905. At Odessa in 1905, 500 Jews were murdered. Dmitri Tolstoy, the Minister of the Interior, tried to replace this disorder with a more systematic policy. Jews were forbidden to trade on Christian holy days; they could not settle in the rural areas, they were not allowed to take up any more than 10 per cent of school or university places. Expulsion of 'illegal' settler Jews in Moscow and St Petersburg was encouraged. As a result of this harassment, some Jews formed a Zionist organisation called the Bund (1897), which mutated into revolutionary socialist action in the twentieth century.

Economic problems

Economic reforms were difficult when Russia was poor and its leaders feared change

Although Russia had abundant resources, it lacked capital to develop and exploit them. Russia's infrastructure was especially poor. Worse still, there were many who feared the consequences of industrialisation. The conservative élites believed that it would create disruptive social forces that would destroy the old order in Russia. When Sergei Witte was appointed Minister of Finance and Commerce in 1892, the government's policy changed. Witte was convinced that Russia would only remain a Great Power if it could take its place amongst the leading industrial nations of the world. He believed the Russian government had to guide that development. What is immediately apparent is the difference in Russia from the development of the countries of Western Europe. In the West, entrepreneurs, private companies and banks drove industrialisation. State intervention was frowned upon as restrictive and free enterprise was the rallying cry of capitalism. Witte was advocating a state-directed industrialisation programme, but, unless he was able to generate a spirit of capitalism and enlarge the middle classes, this development would not be easily sustained.

Witte's measures were a partial success

Witte knew that Russia lacked the capital to develop itself and the rouble was too weak to compete with other currencies. This was evident when, after low tariffs had caused an influx of foreign goods, Russia raised high protective tariffs in 1891. As a result, foreign loans were brought in, especially from France. Unfortunately, to pay the interest the government increased direct taxation (thus avoiding a damaging direct income tax of the wealthy) and this burden fell heavily on the peasants. Russia also adopted the gold standard (1897) to give greater prestige to the currency. Some of the foreign capital was spent on the development of the railway network, the most efficient of all transport systems then available. Before 1892, annual railway construction had been limited to 400 miles a year. In the 1890s, that increased to 1,400 miles a year. However, despite this spectacular increase, most of the expansion was in a single line, the Trans-Siberian Railway, which was begun in 1891 and completed in 1902. Given the vast size of Russia, the railway network density was still low compared with other countries (the USA had 411,000 km but Russia had only 62,000 in 1913). In addition, some lines were still being built for military rather than economic purposes such as the line across Turkestan in Central Asia, although industrial areas were now being linked. Witte urged the development of heavy industries as a catalyst to other economic development, namely iron, steel, cotton, oil, coal and the machine industries. Under Witte's leadership coal production doubled and there were great leaps in other areas, but from such a low starting point, these figures still lagged behind the West. His factory regulations and control of liquor were designed to discipline the workforce.

Problems in the Russian economy continued

Peasant farmers found themselves as impoverished at the turn of the century as their forefathers had been. Low bread prices were fixed by the government, but this meant low rates of return for the farmers and particular hardship when the harvests failed as they did in 1891, 1892, 1898 and 1901. Peasant holdings were often small and inefficient and so, when the population of Russia began to rise, the pressure on existing land ownership grew intolerable. The average land tenure in 1877 had been 35 acres, but this fell to 28 acres in 1905. Poverty, 'land hunger', arrears in taxation payments and under-investment continued to plague the agrarian economy. The government's first concern was to strengthen the nobility as the basis of political support for the régime. To alleviate their indebtedness, Land Banks were established in 1886. These were backed by government funds and former state lands that could be purchased by the peasants themselves at favourable rates, sometimes as low as 4 per cent. In addition, new 'virgin lands' were exploited. In 1896, the Resettlement Bureau was established to encourage migration to Siberia. Criminals ceased to be shipped there in 1900 and by that same year some 750,000 peasants had moved. However, the number of peasants in Russia exceeded 97 million in 1895 so the migrations barely kept pace with the natural increase. Peasant land ownership did increase by 26 million hectares in the years 1877–1905, but much land was still privately owned.

Russian agriculture lacked modernisation

The centre of village decision-making was the *Mir*, and its imposed restrictions on travel and discouraged innovation. Poverty meant that there was little land improvement. Most farming methods were the same as those of medieval times. In 1900, an average acre of Russian land produced 8.8 bushels of wheat, compared with 13.9 in the United States and 35.4 in Great Britain. Although Russia was exporting millions of tonnes of grain each year by 1913, it did so in order to pay for capital investment in industry and at the expense of its people. Witte was dismissed because of the 1905 Revolution in Russia, but his successor, Piotyr Stolypin, continued Witte's industrial policies. Yet Stolypin is also associated with the régime's attempts to create a loyal peasantry. His hard repression during the 1905 disturbances was to be matched by a solution of the agrarian backwardness that was creating discontent. He made it legal for any peasant to withdraw from the commune in 1906 and in 1910 he dissolved all communes that had failed to redistribute land since the Edict of Emancipation. Stolypin also introduced civil rights in local administration (1906) and he allocated more state land to the Peasants' Land Bank the same year to alleviate the land hunger.

Stolypin also failed to solve the agrarian crisis

By 1905, some 20 per cent of the peasantry owned their own land and by 1915 this had risen to 50 per cent. Attempts at consolidation of smaller plots into larger farms were less successful, running at 10 per cent by the outbreak of war. Three million cases were still waiting to be resolved when the war broke out. Lower interest rates at the Land Banks and the migration of more peasants to Siberia were also attempts to solve the problems in agriculture. However, it was probably a case of 'too little, too late'. Despite some evidence of success, the intervention of the war brought the countryside to a state of crisis. Even before the war, Stolypin was falling foul of the Tsar and the right-wing ministers that surrounded him. He was about to be dismissed when he was assassinated by a double agent called Bogrov. Mystery has always surrounded the motives of a man who was working for both the Social Revolutionaries' terrorist movement and the state's secret police. Could Stolypin have ever created a loyal mass of conservative land-owning peasants? Historical examples from across Europe refute the idea that land ownership automatically produced loyalty to any régime. In 1905, and again in 1917, some of the most violent disturbances occurred in the countryside.

Russia on the eve of revolution

The Social Democratic Party believed revolution was the solution to Russia's ills

There were many discontented groups in Russia before the First World War. Urban workers (the proletariat), endured long hours, low pay and sometimes dangerous working conditions. Overcrowded slum accommodation added to the misery. Yet to these somewhat typical industrial problems were added the inequalities of the political system. The Russian people were deprived of a voice for their grievances. Intellectuals and the middle class were as disgruntled as the seething masses of the cities and the countryside. Only a devotion to the Tsar seemed to keep the country together. The Social Democratic Party, most of whom lived in exile, believed the solution was for Russia to pass through this period of industrialisation, for the workers to develop a sense of class consciousness (an awareness of their misery that bonded them together in class solidarity) and to effect a revolution. Unfortunately, the proletariat in Russia were heavily outnumbered by the peasantry who, it was thought, would always side with the Tsar. Most of the party was prepared to wait until the conditions in Russia matched those outlined by Karl Marx as prerequisites for a successful revolution. Martov hoped to see the peasant enlisted as part of a popular movement that would sweep away the régime, but Vladimir Illyich Lenin disagreed.

Lenin wanted 'two revolutions in one' led by a Red Guard

Lenin argued that the bourgeoisie in Russia, although small, would try to overthrow the Tsar just as other middle-class movements had done in the West. At that moment, he believed the proletariat must immediately make their own bid for power, whilst there was still confusion. However, to prevent the forces of order uniting against the workers, Lenin advocated the formation of a Red Guard, a professional force of revolutionaries who could lead and organise the proletariat. Lenin argued with Martov that the peasantry could have no role in a revolution. Disagreements in the Social Democratic Party led to a split in 1903. Lenin's smaller faction was ironically called the Bolsheviks (the 'majority men') and Martov's larger group was called the Mensheviks (the 'minority'). Both sides nevertheless tended to reject acts of terrorism in favour of a concerted propaganda campaign.

The Social Revolutionaries were the most significant group of the period

Although the Marxists under Lenin were eventually successful, it is easy to forget that, before the war, the most important resistance group were the Social Revolutionaries or SRs (formed 1901). They inherited the Populist tradition, being made up of students who saw Russia's future in the solution of the land question. They advocated the nationalisation of the land, but focused on terrorist activity and helped agitate unrest in rural areas in 1902. Lionel Kochan has pointed out the ambiguity of some of their ideas, for there were some who favoured the urban workers as a revolutionary force. Thus the official party programme envisaged a peasant rebellion spearheaded by the urban proletariat. It was the growth of terrorism though that caused the Minister of the Interior, Phleve, to remark in 1903: 'What this country needs is a short, victorious war to stem the tide of revolution'.

The 1905 Revolution illustrated the extent of Russia's problems

The 1905 Revolution was sparked by the humiliating defeat of Russia in the Russo-Japanese War, but it was also the culmination of years of unrest. In 1902, there had been a series of peasant riots, followed by a string of industrial disputes and student demonstrations. The Chief of Police in Moscow had experimented in the control of this unrest by the introduction of 'police socialism' in 1902. It attempted to meet demands for improvements in hours and wages in order to avoid more violent outrages. The most successful organisation that was set up under this scheme was the Assembly of Russian Factory Workers, which attracted 8,000 workers in just one year. It was led by Father Gapon. When Gapon accompanied a march to the Winter Palace in St Petersburg on 22 January 1905, the crowd swelled to 150,000. The advance of this multitude panicked the armed police cordon and they opened fire. There are estimates that as many as 1,000 were killed and wounded. More than any other incident, 'Bloody Sunday' undermined the authority of Tsarism in the eyes of ordinary people. A strike wave followed, with 2.7 million workers protesting by 1906. The strike of the railway workers was arguably the most damaging, with cities brought to the verge of starvation.

Unrest spread to the peasants and the armed forces

In February 1905, the first serious peasant unrest began in the Kursk region, but this quickly spread to the rest of European Russia. The All-Russian Peasant Union articulated their demands, but this was little more than a front organisation for the SRs since its demands were identical to the terror groups'. Most of the rioting involved local revenge on landowners and property. Troops were deployed to the 3,228 most serious incidents. Yet the position of the armed forces was crucial in the disturbances. With some of the best units away in the Far East fighting Japan, some units mutinied and navy crews at Kronstadt refused to co-operate. The most famous mutiny was that of the battleship *Potemkin*, where the men killed some of their officers and shelled Odessa before giving themselves up in Romania. The régime curbed the military disturbances by using non-Russian troops to put down Russian rioters and vice versa. Promises of better pay and conditions also won over many soldiers and sailors.

The *Dumas* offered a chance for democracy in Russia

Some liberal thinkers formed themselves into the Constitutional Democratic Party ('Kadets') in October 1905, and they demanded an elected assembly based on universal suffrage. On the left, revolutionary groups were taken by surprise by the events of 1905. In St Petersburg, for example, no revolutionaries played any part in the spontaneous emergence of the first *Soviet* (Council) made up of 500 men from 96 separate trade unions. Nevertheless, Leon Trotsky (real name, Lev Bronstein) soon captured the imagination of many workers with his skilful oratory, and the *Soviet* became Menshevik in outlook. In November, the *Soviet* tried to co-ordinate a second general strike (the first was in October), but it failed. The Tsar took the sting out of the political demands by promising a *Duma* (assembly) in the October Manifesto. It also offered freedom of speech, of assembly, of conscience and liberty for the individual. Those liberals who accepted the terms were known as Octoberists, but some expected further concessions from the Tsar. However, in November, the Tsar cancelled peasant redemption payments and called on them to return to peace and order.

The concessions of 1905 were a sham

When the army began to restore order and troops started to return from the Far East, the Tsar acted against the revolutionaries. The leaders of the Union of Peasants and the St Petersburg *Soviet* were arrested. In December, an insurrection in Moscow, in which some Bolsheviks played a minor part, was destroyed with the loss of 1,000 lives. Far-right groups, such as the Union of the Russian People and terror gangs called the 'Black Hundreds' lynched reformers and stirred up anti-Semitic propaganda. This set a precedent. The more the revolutionaries fought back with terrorism and assassination (2,999 died in these murders), the more the new premier, Stolypin, responded with counter-terror. Field Courts Martial were established and 1,144 people were executed. Newspapers and unions were closed down. Worse still, the Tsar passed the Fundamental Laws just before the opening of the first *Duma* in May 1906. The Tsar retained his autocratic powers, including control of foreign policy, the executive, and the armed forces. An upper house, the Council of the Empire, would give its consent to any bills offered by the *Duma*, but the Tsar selected half its members. The Tsar could appoint and dissolve the *Duma*, and rule by decree when it was not in session.

The *Dumas* failed but were significant in their very existence

The first *Duma* was dominated by the Kadets, but their demands that the upper house be made responsible to the *Duma*, and that crown lands should be given to the peasants merely compelled the Tsar to dissolve the whole assembly. When some of the Kadets went to Finland and urged people not to pay taxes until their demands were met (the Vyburg Manifesto), they were denied the right to re-election. The government tried to interfere with the elections of the second *Duma* but about a quarter of the delegates were radicals, including 54 Social Revolutionaries and 34 Social Democratic Party men. The second *Duma* lasted three months. A new electoral law restricted the franchise and the third *Duma* was more conservative, being made up mainly of landowners and industrialists. The *Duma* lasted until 1913 and was replaced by a fourth. These conservative *Dumas* co-operated with Stolypin. The most important reform they managed was a

welfare measure that introduced accident and health insurance in 1912. The
Land Commandants were also replaced with Justices of the Peace, and, in
conjunction with the local *zemstva*, there were improvements in elementary
education. By 1914, half of Russian children (7.2 million) were getting an
education. Indeed, Hugh Seton-Watson believed that the *Dumas* represented a
truly democratic advance when, before 1905 the existence of an assembly whose
dealings were published in the press, was unthinkable.

Foreign policy

Russia had remained in isolation since the Crimean War, and the treatment of the
Polish Revolt did nothing to improve her international reputation. Yet, in the mid
1860s, Tsar Alexander II began a new phase of expansion into the Caucasus,
Central Asia and the Far East. Local commanders exceeded their orders from St
Petersburg, but spoils were generously rewarded. The fabled cities of Tashkent,
Bokhara and Samarkand were quickly absorbed. Whilst this brought him under
the suspicion of Great Britain, a rival power in Asia, all the operations were
ultimately successful. In 1872, Bismarck's eagerness to keep France isolated
brought Russia into the *Dreikaiserbund*, an entente that turned into a formal
military alliance in 1881. However, in 1877 and 1878, attempts to influence the
Balkans ended in a disastrous war against Turkey and a humiliating peace deal at
the Congress of Berlin (see Chapter 4). The limits of Russia's eastward expansion
were also defined. Russia sold Alaska to the United States in 1867, and the
development of the Far Eastern port of Vladivostok was dependent on the
completion of the Trans-Siberian Railway. However, this new expansion aroused
the hostility of Japan, who feared that Korea would be the next to be annexed.
Russia confirmed this suspicion when it compelled the Japanese to relinquish the
Laiotung Peninsula after the Sino-Japanese War of 1894–95, only to seize the land
for itself in 1898. When Manchuria fell under Russian influence, the Japanese
prepared for a lightning war.

The Russo-Japanese War and the consequences of defeat

The Japanese launched a surprise attack on Port Arthur to neutralise the Russian
Pacific Fleet. After a long siege, the port fell. Russia had immense difficulties
reinforcing its Far Eastern garrison as all the troops and supplies had to pass along
the Trans-Siberian railway. As in the Crimea, Russia was finding it difficult to
fight a war on the very periphery of the Empire because of poor logistics and
transport. The Japanese forced the army of General Kuropatkin to withdraw
after a major battle at Mukden (February-March 1905). To cut the Japanese
supply routes, the Russians despatched the Baltic Fleet right round the world, but
its well-publicised voyage ended in May 1905 when it was ambushed by Admiral
Togo's main battle fleet in the Tsushima Strait. The Russians lost 25 out of their
35 vessels to highly trained Japanese gunners. With growing unrest at home, the

Russians were relieved by an American offer of mediation which resulted in the Treaty of Portsmouth. Russia had been humiliated and its weakness fuelled German and Austrian geopolitical ambitions. However, the Russians were more determined than ever to restore their national honour and they sought to challenge Austrian arrogance in the Balkans.

Historical controversies

The Tsars have received a mixed historiography
W.E. Mosse believed that Alexander II couldn't be regarded as a 'liberator'. He was too cut off from the people, and even the conservatives at court were disillusioned with his reforms. Hugh Seton-Watson also believed that Alexander was trying to reach an unrealistic compromise between a constitutional government and an autocracy. By contrast, P.A. Zaionchkovsky was more optimistic, feeling that democracy could have come in Russia had not Alexander been murdered that day in 1881. Yet to make any of the reforms work, Russia lacked a stable economic foundation. In this period, Russia lagged behind the Western powers despite its huge reservoir of resources. Before the Revolution, any writings on the Tsars took the form of sympathetic biographies, and even in recent years there have been attempts to focus on the paternal side of Nicholas II and his relationship with Alexandra, the Tsarina. After 1917, however, Marxist interpretations dominated Russian accounts of the period.

The Marxist interpretations of the past had a modern political agenda
Marxist historians were under pressure to interpret the events before and after the revolution in the narrow criteria of ideology. Lenin instructed, for the purposes of modern political propaganda, that the emphasis should be placed on the heroic role of the proletariat and the inevitability of their victory in 1917. All other groups were diminished in importance in the works of M. Pankratova, Aaron Avrekh and A.B. Shapkarin. The 'optimists' school of thought in the West, seen in the work of A. Gerschenkron, believed that the fall of the Tsars had not been inevitable and that democracy may have flourished but for the war. Theodore von Laue took a 'pessimists' line, concluding that the forces arraigned against democracy were too great. Liberal historians of the West generally have been critical of the brutality and deception of the Bolsheviks, rejecting the 'inevitability' of Soviet victory. However, since the opening of the Soviet archives and the collapse of communism in Russia, the focus has been on re-examining the Soviet era, rather than the period before the revolution. There has been much criticism of the revolutionaries, but equally there has been no attempt to portray the Tsarist system in a more positive light.

Tutorial

Progress questions
1. What were the consequences of the Edict of Emancipation?

2. Why were there so many opposition movements in Russia before 1914?

3. How successful were the economic reforms of Sergei Witte?

4. What was the significance of the 1905 Revolution?

Discussion points
1. Is there any justification for calling Alexander II the 'Tsar Liberator'?

2. Could the 1905 revolution, or indeed the 1917 revolution, have been averted?

Practical assignment
Write an essay of circa 1,000 words in response to the following question: 'Between 1866–1904, the rulers of the Russian Empire were required to deal with insoluble problems, including those of governing so many non-Russians'. Assess the validity of this statement. A suggested answer can be found at the back of the book.

Study and revision tips
1. The key areas of this topic are the land question, the failure of economic reform and the growth of revolutionary groups. Your own notes and reading could be clustered around this topic.

2. Note how the Soviet interpretation of this period differed from the accounts in the West. Be careful not to attribute too much importance to 'inevitability' or the 'proletariat' as these were propaganda inventions. All the revolutionaries, except the Populists and many of the SRs, felt the peasantry had no role to play, but this was an error.

3. Be clear about the definitions of 'revolution': this is a favourite question.

7

Britain, 1870–1914

One-minute summary - In the first half of the nineteenth century, Britain had emerged as the most powerful state in Europe from an economic point of view. Her dominance of world trade and manufacturing, and her naval supremacy, meant that her interests were truly global. Her chief rival, until the 1850s, had been France, but the defeat of France in 1870 neutralised this threat. The second rival, contending for control of Asia, was Russia. By the 1880s, other powers began to catch up with Britain's economic leadership, and, by 1900, America and Germany had surpassed Britain in the production of coal and steel. However, Germany's militaristic bid for influence over Europe, and its challenge to British naval mastery, compelled Britain to settle its differences with France and Russia. On the eve of war, Britain was policing the world's largest Empire, but was faced with industrial, social and (in Ireland) political unrest at home.

In this chapter you will learn:

▶ how the British favoured free trade and industrialisation
▶ the importance of the British Empire
▶ how democratic governments coped with the problems they faced
▶ themes in British foreign policy that concerned Europe
▶ historical controversies.

Free trade and industrialisation

British prosperity was based on the mid-nineteenth century assumption that trade without tariffs was the only way that countries could thrive financially. Free trade represented a form of liberalism that accrued benefits not just to manufacturers but also to consumers. Increasing wealth, it was thought, trickling down to the lower classes, strengthened the people against tyranny. Moreover, it was widely believed that free trade between nations meant that countries were more likely to be co-operative and peaceful. Thus free trade was a route to world peace. Such confidence was based on the rapid industrialisation and prosperity that Britain enjoyed by the mid-nineteenth century. So deep was the faith in free trade that when other countries began to erect protective tariffs and when trade slowed down causing a depression in the 1890s, the British continued to believe that free trade was the right policy. In 1903, the Colonial Secretary Joseph Chamberlain, attempted to steer his Conservative Party towards protectionism, but this cost the Tories the election of December 1905. The Liberals enjoyed their biggest ever landslide on the ticket of preserving free trade. More worrying was the ageing of

British production methods, and the lack of competitiveness in British industry compared with German and American business.

Britain was the world's financial centre

Despite the problems of British manufacturing, the British economy continued to grow and production increased. Consumer demand also grew, even though real wage values fell for the lower classes in the period 1900–1910. The overall trend for the period 1870–1914 was certainly up. Above all, the British economy benefited from being the world's banker. Insurance services, loans, bonds and shares were centred on the City of London. The pound sterling was a respected world currency.

The British Empire

The British Empire was the world's largest empire in history. It covered a fifth of the world's surface and controlled, supervised or directly governed about a quarter of the global population. It had developed over 300 years, and was an assemblage of different forms of state and government: devolved constitutional government in Australia, rule through intermediaries in West Africa ('trustee-ship') and vice regal authoritarianism in India. The Empire provided Britain with a reservoir of resources, from palm oil on the Gold Coast to frozen lamb in New Zealand, and also a pool of manpower for Britain's armed forces. Across the Empire's shipping lanes, on islands or on the tips of greater land masses, there were smaller outposts and ports. Patrolling these was the Royal Navy and ploughing back and forth was a giant merchant fleet. Handfuls of missionaries, civil service officials, teachers, planters, soldiers, wives, doctors and governors were spread between the millions of indigenous peoples. The British felt they brought with them order and stability, medicine, and improvement, civilisation and Christianity. Their critics accused them of conquest, unjust rule and racism. The Colonies of Settlement, Australia, New Zealand, Canada and South Africa, were seen rather differently from the other colonies. These were 'Greater Britain', a part of the United Kingdom extended into the world like America's westward expansion or Russia's drive across Siberia.

Democratic governments

Britain was regarded as a model democracy by European liberals

Britain was unique amongst the nations of the world in the extent of its democracy. Its constitutional monarchy served the purpose of head of state but had little power. Power and authority lay in Parliament with its elected House of Commons and a hereditary peerage in the House of Lords. A Cabinet, formed from one of two main political parties, initiated policy. Elections were held every seven years, thus making the government accountable to the people. Rights and freedoms were enshrined in law, but the democratic system itself was based on precedent. This had the effect of ensuring continuity and avoided too radical a shift in the constitution. Britain was regarded as the mother of parliaments and with some justification, Britons sang that they would 'never be slaves' and that Britain was the 'mother of the free' in the ever-popular *Rule Britannia*. In 1832, the Great Reform Act had widened the franchise to include the middle classes and in 1867 the Second Parliamentary Reform Act gave the vote to propertied members of the working class. Along with the development of a mass media and cheap consumer products, the era of mass politics had dawned.

There was a wave of social reform in the wake of the Second Reform Act
To meet the aspirations of the new electorate, a large number of reforms were passed to improve the working and living conditions of the labouring classes, and to meet the aspirations of the middle classes. Education was made free and compulsory at primary level in 1870. Secondary education lagged behind, but there were significant improvements in public schools (private, fee-paying education). However, their emphasis on sport and discipline, or the classical languages and ancient history, has been criticised because it neglected technical and industrial skills. Recommendations were made to extend the secondary system, but in 1907 only 25 per cent of secondary school places were offered to the working classes. In 1902, the conflicting private and school controls over secondary education were streamlined by the creation of Local Education Authorities, but attempts to raise the school leaving age to 14 were shelved in 1917. It was not until 1944 that secondary education became free for all. At the higher education level, universities were independent and unrestricted by government. Women could became undergraduates when Girton College Cambridge opened in 1873. Equally significant were the improvements in conditions in the cities: parks, public baths, street lighting, sanitation, water supply and public transport.

The era was characterised by party politics
Fierce competition developed between the two leading parties, the Conservatives and the Liberals. The Conservatives held that the established institutions of state should be conserved where good and reformed where necessary and they favoured monarchy, imperialism, law and order and the defence of property. The Liberals contained elements that were almost conservative in outlook (the Whigs), but also radicals who looked for progressive reforms, giving more power to the people, reforming institutions, preserving peace and cutting state expenditure. The Conservative leader of the 1870s, Benjamin Disraeli, and the Liberal leader of the same period, William Gladstone were bitter enemies, the former flamboyant in style and the latter deeply religious and austere. Disraeli died in 1881 and was replaced by the patrician Lord Salisbury. Under his leadership, and then his

nephew Arthur Balfour, the Tories dominated British politics until 1905. This was because two issues split the Liberal party: self-government for Ireland, and the future of the British Empire.

Ireland was the main issue of the late-nineteenth century
Ireland had been incorporated into the United Kingdom in 1800, but the majority Catholic peasant population were engaged in inefficient forms of agriculture. When blight struck the staple potato crop in the 1840s, starvation and malnutrition resulted. The process of migration from the land to the cities, as agricultural methods changed, had taken place over centuries in Britain, but in Ireland the landowners needed to eject poor tenants from the land rapidly because land values fell and the only way to sustain revenues was to consolidate land and modernise methods. The eviction of peasants from the land was thus telescoped into a few decades, causing a more acute dislocation of Irish society. Without the industrial revolution in Ireland to absorb the surplus, many fled to British cities or to America. Not all were prepared to change. Irish nationalists pursued a campaign for self-government, or Home Rule, in parliament, but also fanned the flames of agitation in Ireland. In 1882, Charles Parnell was practically encouraging the extremists by his inflammatory speeches. He only moderated his attacks when he was gaoled and feared terrorists would take over his movement. Gladstone tried to conciliate and attempted to give Ireland Home Rule, but not all his party followed him and the party divided in 1886.

The Empire was regarded as essential for the future
Those that split from the Liberal Party over Ireland were known as Liberal Unionists (because they wanted to maintain the union of Britain and Ireland), but they identified with the Conservative belief that the future of Britain as a world power lay in the development of an empire. There was a fear that the loss of Ireland would mean the break up of the Empire, with subject peoples demanding self-government (much as the Americans had done in 1775–83), so the two issues were linked. Whilst the Empire did not produce many resources, it was thought that, in time, the British would be able to develop the colonies and its plantations, minerals and consumer demand. Earl Rosebery, the Liberal leader of 1894 stated: 'we are pegging out claims for the future'. However, most colonies that were acquired in the late nineteenth century were only partially related to economic potential. The scramble between the Great Powers for imperial territories made the British feel they needed to defend their interests. With a small army and a collection of naval stations, this would mean the annexation of hinterlands. Governments resented the expense of running colonies and wanted to minimise costs, so colonies were acquired 'reluctantly'. J.R. Seeley, a Cambridge University lecturer, believed the Empire was acquired 'in a fit of absence of mind' as it came together without any unifying strategy, but he urged the British people to recognise their new global role as the future trajectory of the nation.

The South African War caused some reflection in Britain

A conflict which began in 1899 as another colonial war, was soon marked by a series of setbacks for the British. Reinforcements were poured into southern Africa and the British army eventually overran the two Boer Republics of the Orange Free State and the Transvaal in 1900. The town of Mafeking, which had held out for months, was relieved in May and the British public used the moment to celebrate, with a sense of relief, that honour and imperial prestige had been preserved. However, the war was far from over as Boers formed themselves into small guerrilla squads called Commandoes and harassed railway lines and supply columns. To win the war, General Kitchener cleared the land of civilians and crops that could supply the Boer fighters. Overcrowded 'concentration' camps were swept by disease and British humanitarians were shocked at the death toll. A pro-Boer lobby criticised the government, but the majority remained steadfast in their support of the British war effort. More disquieting was the feeling that the war had been difficult to win. The state of the British recruits who had been presented for duty was shocking too: many were turned away as malnourished. There was speculation that the neglect of the lower classes was actually causing the 'degeneration' of the race.

New Liberalism and Labour heralded a new era in British politics

To deal with the nation's health and apparent inefficiency, the Liberals were returned to power with a new willingness to implement reforms. They advocated state intervention to create a minimum standard of care and support for the disadvantaged of society. Pensions were introduced in 1909. In 1911, National Insurance for health and accident at work was brought in. Children were given free school meals and medical inspections. Yet, to many labouring men, a minimum standard was not enough. Trade unionists joined with radical activists to form the Labour Party in 1906. They lobbied for further reform in parliament, but lacked the numbers to make a significant impact on the two leading parties. Between 1910 and 1913, trade union unrest resulted in serious rioting and four died, but concessions to miners and to the Labour Party, coupled with an economic upswing, quelled the disturbances. However, some middle-class women were less easily assuaged. The militant suffragettes conducted a campaign of civil disobedience and hunger strikes, but they failed to secure the vote for women at national level. In Ireland, the reform of the British House of Lords (which lost its power to block legislation in 1911), led to the reintroduction of a Home Rule Bill. Private armies were formed by Protestant Ulstermen who refused to accept the rule of a southern Irish, Catholic parliament (Dail) or severance from Britain. Nationalists also armed themselves, making a civil war likely. The outbreak of war prevented the catastrophe and Irishmen on both sides joined up to fight for the King-Emperor.

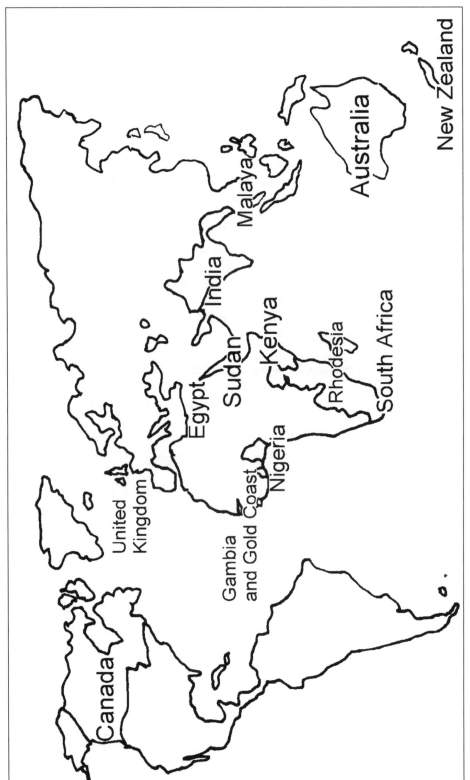

Figure 7. The British Empire in 1870.

Themes in British foreign policy

British statesmen hoped to avoid alliances with other European powers that might lead to commitments to go to war, and thus conflict with Britain's aim to develop trade peacefully. War, it was thought, was bad for business. Instead of formal alliances, the British sought understandings and agreements. They aimed to settle their differences through diplomacy. Nevertheless, the threats to the sprawling British Empire seemed to multiply as others acquired empires in the late nineteenth century and Britain could not be strong everywhere at once. The chief rivals were France and Russia, mainly because of their proximity to British possessions in Africa or Asia, and conflicting claims over unoccupied territories in West Africa, Afghanistan or South-East Asia. Once the scramble for territory in Africa and Asia had begun to slow down, Britain hoped for a preservation of the *status quo*. It was particularly concerned to avoid one power becoming dominant over Europe, and therefore developing into a threat to Britain's shores. Salisbury signed the Mediterranean Agreements to keep the territorial position in southern Europe the same. In a similar vein, Britain formed an alliance with Japan in 1902 to preserve the balance of power in the Far East. The Foreign Secretaries Lord Lansdowne (Conservative) and Sir Edward Grey (Liberal) settled older disputes with France in 1904 and Russia in 1907.

Diplomacy with Germany failed

However, attempts to negotiate with Germany failed. The development of a revolutionary new battleship design in 1906 sparked off a naval race, and the Kaiser's aggressive diplomacy angered British politicians. In 1906 and again in 1912, the British held secret talks with the French on their deployments in the event of a war with Germany. Britain's concerns were consistent throughout: that no single power should dominate Europe, trade routes and the Empire must be protected, and the home waters should remain under the control of the Royal Navy.

Historical controversies

Paul Kennedy argued that Britain's foreign policy was inherently conservative in this period, and it could be said that there was little difference in the two parties' approach to the British Empire and to international relations. British foreign policy was driven by a desire to protect British interests and that meant the defence of the United Kingdom, its possessions and its trade. Commerce was the basis of British prosperity and the outbreak of war threatened the circulation of trade. It is noticeable that, of all the European powers in 1914, only Britain's Sir Edward Grey refused to be resigned to war. When he failed to preserve peace, he remarked prophetically: 'The lamps are going out all over Europe – We shall not see them lit again in our lifetime'.

There was less consensus at home

At home, political differences were more acute. The sincerity or politicking of Gladstone and Disraeli has been debated by biographers of both men (such as H.C. Matthew for Gladstone and Lord Blake for Disraeli), although most are convinced that, showmanship aside, they genuinely believed in the principles they stood for. Gradually, the two dominant parties, which had passed a flurry of reforms in 1870s, had to acknowledge the existence of pressure from Irish and Labour MPs. Dissatisfied with the continuation of substantial reform in the 1880s and 1890s, the two groups pursued their agendas through a more sympathetic Liberal Party. However, the Conservatives, who had been roundly defeated in 1905, soon regained support from a British electorate alarmed by radicalism. Thus whilst Henry Pelling considers the rise of Labour as an inevitable outcome of working-class politics, P.F. Clarke highlights the relative insignificance of the pre-war Labour movement. In the same way, George Dangerfield's belief that Liberal England suffered a 'strange death' at the hands of working class radicalism is challenged by the evidence from Trevor Wilson, to the effect that the Liberal Party was still a going concern before the First World War, but a split during the war damaged its reputation at a crucial time.

Tutorial

Progress questions

1. Why did the main political parties scramble to pass reforms in the 1870s?

2. What were the reasons for denying Ireland self-government between 1885 and 1914?

3. What principles guided British foreign policy before the First World War?

Discussion points

1. Why, given Britain's industrial and imperial might, were British statesmen so concerned by the prospect of war?

2. How might other European powers have viewed Britain between 1870 and 1914?

Practical assignment

Using a map of the British Empire, identify, and account for, those areas about which British statesmen were anxious. Annotate these summaries on to the border of the map.

Study and revision tips

1. Consider constructing a wire diagram or mind map to summarise Britain's history in this period. Notice how Britain responded to the imperialism of others. As Britain's early industrial lead slipped, and others caught up, it easy to see why some people were anxious about the future.

2. To find out more about Britain in this period, see *British History 1870–1918* in the Studymates series.

3. Do not try to remember all the names and details of British policies covered in this chapter. Use this information on Britain to make a comparison with other European countries. Britain's political system was regarded as the most enlightened in Europe; consider how that would affect foreign relations.

8

Italy, 1870–1914

One-minute summary – Italy was united in 1861, with Venetia and Rome being added in 1866 and 1870 respectively. This young nation was nevertheless still divided by the poverty of the south compared with the industrialised north, the hard-pressed workers against the employers, the Papacy against the secular Italian state, the provinces against the central government, but worst of all, by the anger of the people with their politicians. The damaging experience of changing coalitions and short-lived ministries and the corruption of politicians, meant that faith in parliamentary democracy was limited. Throughout the period, there were frequent episodes of violent unrest and a general strike took place in 1904. The workers did not just down tools, but migrated from Italy in vast numbers too, a process described as a 'haemorrhage' of its workforce. The growing support for extremists of the left appeared to be the greatest threat to the future of the liberal Italian state, but an embryonic nationalist movement that placed its faith in war and action laid the foundations of the far right politics of the 1920s.

In this chapter you will learn:

▶ how the legacy of unification affected Italy
▶ why Liberal governments dominated Italian politics
▶ what domestic problems faced Italy
▶ the changing relations of the Italian state and the Papacy.

The legacy of unification

When Italy was unified in 1861, it had been through the combined efforts of the republican revolutionary leader Guiseppe Garibaldi and the Prime Minister of Piedmont, Count Camillo di Cavour. In 1860, Garibaldi had 'liberated' southern Italians from the oppressive rule of the Neapolitan rulers, with a band of volunteers called the 'Thousand Redshirts'. This romantic figure had captured the imagination of the southerners and he was greeted with enthusiasm. Cavour, by contrast, was a politician of *realpolitik* (the power-politics of realism). He had marched an army through the northern states, apparently to prevent Garibaldi throwing the whole peninsula into anarchy. Yet he had received Garibaldi's gesture of handing over southern Italy with magnanimity. When the first Italian parliament met in Turin on 17 March 1861, it was noticeable that it was in a Piedmontese city. Victor Emmanuel II, the King of Piedmont, became the first King of Italy and, unsurprisingly, Cavour was the Prime Minister. The Piedmontese had begun a ruthless centralisation under their leadership almost

Figure 8. The Italian States.

immediately, ignoring the customs and personnel of the south entirely. Whilst the Italian state was to be a constitutional monarchy, it was to be a highly centralised one under Piedmontese leadership.

The remaining areas of Italy were secured between 1866 and 1871

There were several attempts to regain Venetia from Austria as the last large province of Italians still outside the kingdom. Diplomatic overtures came to nothing, and an offer to purchase the province for 1,000 million lire also failed because the military advisors at the Austrian court thought it would tarnish the

Empire's honour. The Italian states had tried to liberate Venetia by force in 1859, but after their French allies had suffered heavy casualties at Magenta and Solferino, the war had been ended. However, in 1866, the Italians allied themselves with Prussia in the Seven Weeks War. Italian troops were defeated at Custozza and at sea in the battle of Lissa, but their Prussian allies compelled the Austrians to relinquish Venetia. Rome, the nominated capital, had also been outside the kingdom throughout the 1860s, but its French garrison finally abandoned the Papal army in 1870 (on the outbreak of the Franco-Prussian War). Italian troops entered the city, although the Vatican was the retained as the preserve of the Pope. Yet, despite the territorial unity of Italy, the people of Italy did not yet feel united.

Liberal governments

There were deep divisions between north and south
Cavour died in June 1861 and never got to see the final fruits of his labours. No man of his calibre seemed able to resolve the problems of disunity amongst Italians. D'Azeglio, a colleague of Cavour, had remarked: 'We have made Italy; now we have to make Italians'. Major obstacles stood in the way of this aspiration. Indeed, by 1866, there was virtually a civil war in Sicily. Southerners resented the people of the north, whilst northerners sometimes thought of southerners as little more than 'Africans'. Anger at taxation and control by northerners led to a revival of brigandage in the south. Sixty battalions of troops were deployed to keep order, rising to 90,000 men in 1863, but the combination of the right and left wing in Sicily led to a full-scale revolt there. Secret societies and gangs, like the Mafia, terrorised the peasants and extorted their own criminal profits.

The south had a different social and economic organisation to the north
The moderate climate, the better soils and the greater abundance of resources meant that the north had developed a stronger industrial base than the south. The south was mainly agrarian, but its poor soils and old-fashioned methods meant that it was inefficient. The hot climate and agricultural lifestyle also meant that the pace of life was slower. There was always great interest in the conspiratorial and family-based power struggle, but no enthusiasm for the competitive industrial approach to 'progress'. With great poverty came high levels of illiteracy, and despite the establishment of elementary education across the country in 1877, the cost of implementing the reform was an insurmountable obstacle. The aristocracy of the south played little part in the politics of the new state, losing an opportunity for leadership and representation of southern interests, but worse was to follow when southerners were deprived of a vote (apart from the plebiscite of 1860 to join the Italian state) by property qualifications until 1912 (universal manhood suffrage for those over 30).

There was political instability and corruption

During the period 1870–1914, there were frequent changes of government which deprived the state of continuity in its policies. Loose coalitions were formed between parties and factions, but they dissolved and were changed over a series of domestic problems. The right wing was generally stronger in the north, whilst the left enjoyed more support in the south, but there was often an undignified scramble for office. Bribery and corruption, well established in the old politics of the south, were transferred to the new national government where the influence was greater. The buying of votes amongst different factions was common. This process of change in government through corruption was called *transformismo*. Intrigue was common, and local crises or special interests became political currency rather than the greater issues facing the country as a whole.

Domestic problems

The Italian state was poor

The most significant problem was debt. Cavour had run up huge debts by participating in wars in the Crimea and against Austria in 1859. The smaller states brought their own debts to the new Italian state government. A programme of road and rail construction and the building of a large navy added to the burden which was to be resolved through taxation and through foreign loans. These loans carried huge interest payments; a third of Italy's Gross National Product was used to pay off these debts. Foreigners held most railway shares and a third of Italy's bonds.

There was a growth of socialism and violence before the First World War

Given the resentment of northerners in the south, and the lack of real progress through a lack of resources and national wealth, the poorer classes of Italy were prone to the appeal of socialist ideas. This reached its peak in the 1890s, and especially in 1893 in Sicily when serious unrest developed. In 1898, the army was deployed to deal with rioting. In 1900, King Humbert was assassinated, and in the period 1901–1904, there was a spate of riots, strikes and bombings. Many were angry at the political corruption, and the inaction over poverty or poor living and working conditions. Denied a voice through trade unions (they were illegal), there was no other way to express their anger than through direct action. In 1894, new laws clamped down on socialist and anarchist groups, which seemed to worsen the violence in the short term. Without a vote, Italians of the lower classes could not influence politics, but the abysmal performance of Italian troops in the colonial campaign in Abyssinia (where an army was destroyed by native forces) in 1896, sharpened the feelings of national humiliation still further.

Solutions were sought to the violence through both firmness and conciliation

Giovanni Giolitti was a leading left-wing politician during the period 1898–1914.

He introduced old age pensions in 1898, before going on to pass reforms in factory conditions, public health, national insurance and the abolition of child labour. Giolitti did not abandon *transformismo*, but utilised it. He also took firm measures against agitators. In 1898, he introduced martial law and imposed harsh sentences through courts martial. In 1902, he neutralised a railway strike by calling up reservists (many of whom were the strikers, thus placing them under military discipline). Even the Pope lent his support by allowing Catholics to engage in politics to 'preserve order' in 1903. However, these facts reinforce the impression that Italian politicians lacked sincerity when it came to political principle. *Transformismo*, they argued, was the only way to actually govern such diverse and divided groups, but it appears that there was an opportunity to gain and retain personal power and fortunes there too. As Denis Mack Smith noted: 'it was a common refuge where they laid aside their internal quarrels and joined in parcelling out power and jobbery'.

The record of liberal governments in Italy was unimpressive

The leading Liberal politicians, Agostono Depretis (1881–87), Francesco Crispi (1887–90, 1893 and 1896) and Giovanni Giolitti (1892, 1903–04, 1906 and 1911), failed to command much respect, despite their reforms. For example, a series of laws for improvements to agriculture between 1897–1906 failed to prevent a diaspora of 6 million (out of a population of 41 million) labouring men and women to other countries, many of them to the United States. By 1914, 25 per cent of Italians were supporting alternative socialist parties, although the divisions amongst these groups (especially those that supported gradual change, revolution, anarchism or syndicalism) meant they could not secure power. On the nationalist right, the influential writer Gabriele D'Annunzio recaptured the spirit of the *Risorgimento* (unification) particularly after the Italians acquired Libya from Turkey by war in 1911–12. The cost and poor management of the war further discredited the liberal parties, and enhanced the reputation of the belligerent nationalists. The editor of the socialist newspaper *Avanti!*, Benito Mussolini, broke with socialism in the light of D'Annunzio's pronouncements and the collapse of an attempted general strike called *Bieno Rosso* (or 'Red Week') in June 1914. He opposed Italy's neutrality at the outbreak of the war and wanted to see his country participate in an event of great historical significance. Above all, he wanted action, perhaps, as Christopher Hibbert argued, because he thought it would bring forward a revolution and the demise of liberal democracy that he so despised.

Liberal politicians made use of Irrendentism

Italy's political leaders wanted the country to play a role in world affairs and they regarded Italy as a Great Power. However, the nation's military capabilities and its lack of resources meant that other Europeans saw Italy as a second rate power with an important geographical position. Consequently their dealings with Italy were based not on her strength but on her location astride the central Mediterranean. For Italians in the north, the central foreign policy issue was the remaining regions of '*Italia Irredenta*' (Italy unredeemed), a phrase that referred to those areas containing Italians still under Austrian control. The Trentino (South Tyrol) contained 370,000 Italians but its mountainous terrain made it an ideal defensive bulwark for the Habsburg Empire. *Irredentist* agitation sometimes broke out in the region between the Italian workers and the Austrian authorities, and the Italian government looked longingly at the resources available in the area. When Italians in Istria were denied a separate university, anti-Austrian demonstrations broke out in the city of Fiume. Such events helped Italian politicians fan the flames of nationalist sentiment in Italy and thus distract people from domestic problems.

Italian colonialism also served to generate nationalism

Another attempt to match the other European powers and to use foreign policy for domestic purposes was the question of colonialism. Concerned by the emigration of so many Italians to the United States or South America, there was a hope to create colonies in North Africa which would be linked to the mainland. This would revive the glories of the ancient Roman Empire, give business new markets and resources, and, by adding territory to Italy, give others the impression she was a Great Power. Italy first tried to acquire Tunis (a city the Romans had conquered) but France annexed it in 1881. Italy acquired Assab on the Red Sea coast, extending its rule inland over Eritrea. It also took Somaliland on the coast of the Indian Ocean. In 1896, Italy had laid claim to Abyssinia (Ethiopia) but its expedition under General Baratieri was a disaster and amidst great bitterness at home, Ethiopia was effectively independent although designated an 'Italian Protectorate'. However, in 1911–12, Italy got its North African victory and annexed Tripoli (Libya).

The Triple Alliance further enhanced Italy's status

In 1882 Italy joined Germany and Austria to form the Triple Alliance. Anger at the French occupation of Tunis had been the immediate motive, but Italy sought allies to support her colonial ambitions and to avoid international isolation. Extending the existing arrangement with Germany (from 1866) was logical, but linking herself to Austria contradicted the Italian desire to acquire *Italia Irredenta*. However, there were also domestic motives for the alliance. An alliance with Catholic Austria would help to gain the support of the Papacy and prevent intrigues by the Pope against the Italian state (or Austrian influence over Venetia). The alliance would also, it was hoped, make the King more popular and therefore quell republicanism. Germany and Austria welcomed the alliance because it kept France isolated and prevented Italy attacking Austria (which would be important if Germany and Austria ever went to war with Russia).

Italy maintained close links with Great Britain

Rudini, the Italian premier of the 1890s, stated that Britain was the cornerstone of Italy's alliances. Historically, there was a link. The British navy had ensured Garibaldi had been able to cross the Straits of Reggio in 1860 and there had been British volunteers amongst the Thousand Redshirts. The Royal Navy's dominance at sea also protected the Italian peninsula from France. Moreover, Britain supplied the bulk of Italy's coal and iron. Italy had insisted that the Triple Alliance terms must acknowledge that Italy would not fight Britain, a point reiterated when the alliance was renewed in 1890. In the Mediterranean Agreements of 1887, Italy joined Britain in aiming to preserve the *status quo* in the Mediterranean and even offered mutual support for Italian Libya and British Egypt against French designs.

Relations with France gradually improved

Italian claims to Tunis, French support for the Papacy against Italy, tariff wars and membership of the Triple Alliance soured relations between France and Italy in the 1870s and 1880s. However, by the Franco-Italian Convention of 1896, Italy agreed to recognise French rule in Tunis in return for commercial privileges. Two years later a commercial treaty ended the tariff war. A secret agreement in 1900 allowed for Italian recognition of French designs on the future of Morocco, whilst Italy was to be given a free hand against Tripoli. In a further secret treaty of 1902, the Italians agreed to remain neutral in any war against France, which effectively neutralised the Triple Alliance. King Victor Emmanuel visited Paris in 1903 and President Loubert reciprocated in 1904 amidst great popular acclaim.

Italy came to separate agreements with a number of powers

In 1909, Italy signed the Racconigi agreement with Russia which stated that both would try to preserve the *status quo* in the Balkans, Russia would be allowed to open the Straits near Constantinople to her shipping (in the event of a war), and Italy would be given a free hand to operate against Tripoli. The terms reveal a common antagonism with Austria and Turkey, but Italy had agreed not to make agreements with any other power without the participation of Russia and yet, a few days later, Italy made a secret agreement with Austria with very similar terms. Italy was thus not in a position to honour her alliance terms to Austria and Germany, but she did so for practical reasons. Without the strength of the other Great Powers, Italy sought to avoid conflict. This explains her desire to conclude the agreements with Britain and Russia that preserved the *status quo*, or, put another way, the existing balance of power. Italy's agreements were based on self-preservation and naturally on self-interest. Her success against Turkey in 1911–12 was largely a result of this approach to diplomacy.

The relations of the state and the Papacy

The conflict of church and state was heightened by the annexation of Rome

The annexation of the Papal States (provinces under the control of the Pope), by Piedmont in 1860, had turned the Papacy against secular authority in Italy. When Rome was annexed, the Pope, Pius IX, was defiant. He refused to recognise the new Italian state. He called upon Catholics not to participate in the politics of the new regime by the Bull *Non Expedit* (1874). He issued the infamous Bull of Papal Infallibility in July 1870, but its reception amongst Italians was mixed. In the doctrine, the Catholic Church claimed that the Pope spoke with final and supernatural authority on matters of faith and morality. Catholic bishops were empowered to punish non-compliance with excommunication, expulsion from the church or a refusal to permit marriages. However, the Italian state was hardly any more popular on the issue of Rome's annexation. There were disquieting rumours that the plebiscite for Romans to approve of the annexation had been rigged. A French officer in the Papal Army, Comte de Beaufort, alleged that there had been intimidation, an absence of 'no' voting slips, plural voting and the widespread acceptance of unqualified voters. Neither side emerged from the experience free of criticism.

The Italian state tried to conciliate the Pope

The Italian state tried to conciliate the Pope by the Law of Guarantees (1871). The Pope was granted full spiritual jurisdiction across Italy, his communications with Catholics around the world was guaranteed, he was free to appoint the clergy and free of state interference in Catholic education. The Pope also received an annual grant, was not taxed and was given freedom to operate within the Vatican. However, Pius IX described himself as the 'prisoner of the Vatican'.

Pope Leo XIII was prepared to make changes

Pope Leo XIII (1878–1903) took a moderately different line than his predecessor. Although he made no changes to the principles laid down by Pius IX and insisted the church should supervise every aspect of secular life, he was more willing to accept that democracy and monarchy might be able to preserve Catholic principles just as autocracy had apparently done in the past. Leo XIII reached a settlement with the German Chancellor, Bismarck, following years of anti-clericalism, so there was hope that the same could be achieved in Italy. Leo also improved relations with France. Despite the anti-clericalism of the Third Republic, Leo urged French Catholics to break with monarchy and rally to the republic (the *Ralliement*) in 1890. He even persuaded the Tsar to recognise the French republic as a legitimate state. In the Encyclical Rerum Novarum (1891), Leo announced that workers had the right to a just wage, so as to enable them to live and support a family. He applied Christianity to the workplace and urged employers to respond to their moral obligations. It was an important intervention in secular politics.

Pope Pius X permitted Italians to engage in politics but condemned modernity

Pope X was prepared to make small changes to the relationship with the Italian state, but only to benefit the Church. When petitioned by Italian Catholics for approval to enter politics to fight the socialists in 1904, the Pope replied: 'Do as your conscience dictates'. As a result, two Catholic ministers were elected and the socialists lost six seats. However, he refused to embrace modernity (such as democracy) which was denounced as heresy in the encyclical *Vehementer*. He reserved his greatest anger for the French state. His criticised the Republic over the appointment of bishops, he regarded the official visit of the French President, Loubert, in 1904 as a 'grave offence to the sovereign Pontiff', he condemned the anti-clerical laws and excommunicated the French Catholic priest Alfred Loisy for advocating compromise.

Italian politics failed to solve the country's deep-seated problems

The chasm between the Catholic Church and Italian state (which lasted until 1929) was a metaphor for the deep divisions throughout society. The antagonism of north and the south, the provincial loyalties, the unrest in the factories, the distrust of the politicians, and the humiliations in foreign policy were all symptomatic of Italy's political masters' inability to solve the fundamental problem of disunity and poverty. When Italy entered the Great War, the temporary patriotic solidarity masked the new layer of problems the country was burdening itself with. After the war, Italians were disillusioned and they sought solutions from anyone who had the courage to promise improvements, even if that man was Benito Mussolini.

Tutorial

Progress questions

1. What were the chief problems for the Italian state after the *Risorgimento*?

2. Why was there so much political instability in Italy before 1914?

3. How successful was Italian foreign policy after 1870?

4. Why were relations between the Vatican and the Italian government so bad?

Discussion Points

1. 'In every respect, Italy was fundamentally weak.' How far is this true?

2. Did democracy fail in Italy before 1914?

Practical assignment

1. Try to break down the topic by simple comparisons. Take a sheet of paper

and divide it in two. On one side, list the successes of the Italian state and on the other its failures/weaknesses. Try recalling this information by summarising the main headings and then covering them up before writing them out again from memory. Notice how the use of headings can act as memory joggers for the detail.

2. Carry out a similar comparison with other countries like France (democracy) and Austria (autocracy). What broad judgements can you make about how these countries coped with their domestic problems compared with Italy?

Study and revision tips
1. To some extent, Italy between 1870 and 1918 is a less popular topic for historians than the unification of the 1860s and the emergence of fascism after the First World War. However, this period should not be neglected if these other areas are to be fully understood. Conversely, you may find it useful to find out more about the unification and about the rise of fascism so that you can make informed judgements about this period.

2. The conflicts with the Papacy and the divisions of Italian society are the most important aspects of this topic. Notice how foreign policy was conducted with one eye on the domestic effects it would have.

9

New Imperialism

One-minute summary – The nineteenth century was a period when the West projected itself onto the rest of the world to an unprecedented degree, constructing new empires alongside, and sometimes over, far older Asian and African imperial régimes. By 1900 the world was a world of empires. The impulses that drove this expansion were complex and multifaceted, and their effects were no simpler. Europeans sought to restructure the societies they found, they crushed resistance, imposed alien rule and retained exclusive control of power. However, they also introduced new political and philosophical ideas, brought new working practices, developed industries and communications and, in many cases, modernised their colonies. Europeans also rivalled each other, scrambling for resources and regarding neighbours as threatening. They tried to acquire satellite states, buffer zones or strategically valuable terrain, but they also annexed some regions for prestige and popular acclaim. In the process of imperialism, the Europeans suffered setbacks as well as spectacular successes, but the whole episode was relatively short-lived. Most of the European imperial possessions had been relinquished within 80 years of their conquest.

In this chapter you will learn:

▶ the motives for imperialism
▶ the causes of imperial rivalry between the European powers
▶ how Africa was partitioned
▶ how imperialism manifested itself in Asia
▶ the response of the Islamic world
▶ historical controversies.

The motives for imperialism

Economic theories are now less popular as explanations for imperialism

The classic explanation for imperialism was that manufacturing in Europe was reaching a mature stage in its development. Its capacity to produce surpluses led businessmen to seek new outlets to sell their goods beyond Europe. There was also a demand for raw materials, some of which were only available in tropical or sub-tropical regions. These included gold, ivory, oil, rubber and tin. However, there is a problem with this explanation. Businesses didn't want to acquire colonies, but to trade. Taking on the government of a colony was expensive, as the old British East India Company knew well. Errors in government could also cause reactions from the local population, such as the Indian Mutiny of 1857. Businesses preferred to exchange goods. Rarely did government step in to help them. In China, the British government had fought the Chinese in the 1840s to make them trade, but there had been very little occupation (even Hong Kong was leased). In addition, the relative poverty of many nations and peoples outside of Europe meant they lacked the purchasing power to buy large volumes of European products anyway.

Empires may have provided an outlet for surplus capital to be invested
P. Cain and A.G. Hopkins argue that a depression in manufacturing was an incentive to secure guaranteed markets and sources of raw materials outside of Europe. They argued that increasing foreign competition in traditional European and American markets drove the businesses towards the colonies and the developing world. In particular, they point to the growth of financial institutions in Britain and the close connection between them and the imperial government in London; an empire was thus a place to invest surplus capital with a return some time in the future, particularly if other powers raised damaging tariffs.

Empires also developed from older 'bridgeheads'
Coastal toeholds and islands that served as coaling stations or ports were useful places to replenish ships on long journeys. They also provided ports for naval vessels to patrol trade routes and strategic sea-lanes. Local people were employed by Europeans and acted as a link to the hinterlands. John Darwin argued that these older colonial possessions provided the springboard for nineteenth century expansion. Resistance from nomadic or tribal peoples could also draw Europeans into imposing their own order. This became the motive for Russian expansion into Central Asia. Europeans also benefited from the industrialisation of modern weapons. Breech-loading rifles and artillery, and machine guns, enabled small groups of Europeans and their native allies to defeat far larger tribal forces. Technology and research also made it easier for Europeans to combat tropical diseases, with, for example, quinine for malaria.

Exploration and missionaries provided a further impetus for expansion
There was a sense of mission in churches in the mid-nineteenth century to save peoples who had not yet come into contact with the Gospel. There was considerable faith in the benefits of civilisation which the industrial revolution had bestowed on Europe, so that 'Christianity and civilisation' went together as justifications for imperial influence. In Britain, the Victorians had a deep sense of moral duty and a sense of service to others. This was evident in Rudyard Kipling's famous poem *The White Man's Burden*. However, there was a hint of racial supremacy hidden here too, since it was assumed that non-Europeans were incapable of self-improvement and needed European leadership and guidance.

Imperialist ideology was often indistinct
It is hard to identify an imperialist ideology. Britain had a subtle collection of values which coincided with an economic, naval and military superiority in the

early nineteenth century. These values included patriotism, and the status of being a Great Power (where prestige had to be upheld). Disraeli had once argued that an empire would make Britain a cosmopolitan country and a world power, but Liberal critics like Gladstone thought that further expansion was immoral unless it could be demonstrated how benefits might be bestowed on the subject peoples. Sir John Seeley published his *Expansion of England* in 1883 to promote the binding of the colonies of white settlement closer to Britain. Leroy-Beaulieu advocated colonialism in France to reinforce the nation's power. Cain and Hopkins argued that empire offered a way to combat democratic and republican impulses and a way to preserve the privileges of the gentlemen-élites. This puts the cart before the horse in some respects; ideologies actually followed the process of imperialism, they did not lead it. Hence the racial theories of imperialism, such as Herbert Spencer's 'Social Darwinism' (which suggested that races were locked in a struggle for survival that only the fittest nations would survive), and Friedrich Neitzsche's pessimistic belief that only force could solve a nation's struggle, came after the initial period of expansionism.

There were some significant disincentives to expansion

'Informal empire', or influence through existing local élites, was cheaper than outright annexation. Influence could be extended through trade agreements which made client states dependent on the supply of goods from a European state. However, there are problems with this generalisation. Whilst it may appear that Britain controlled many African states and parts of China through 'informal empire', Britain's volume of trade and investment with USA and Argentina was far greater, but the United States cannot be considered part of the British Empire. One quarter of all British investment in 1913 was with Latin America, which were fully independent and resisted any formal controls. Bernard Porter argues that the commercial aspect was only one part of Britain's influence and described the formal empire as 'merely the surface outcrops of a much broader geological reef.' Yet a fear of a loss of financial credit was important to all the European powers. It was necessary to avoid conflict so as not to damage the finances of the country. This was vital in Britain, argued Cain and Hopkins, because British manufacturing was in decline and City finance was progressing. Annexations, they argued, were dictated by the desire to protect property, credit and the flow of trade. As credit was the most important, it was vital to protect it.

There were military factors that curtailed European imperialism

Mountainous frontiers such as the Hindu Kush and Himalaya made further British expansion northwards from India unnecessary, and the jungles on the Burmese frontier made further annexation in that part of Asia difficult. The French control of the Sahara Desert and the rainforests of the Congo were also limited to the peripheries. The risks of a possible defeat at the hands of tribesmen, and a consequent loss of prestige might also deter annexation. In 1881, British forces had been surprised and defeated at Majuba Hill by rebellious Transvaal Boers. Gladstone had given the rebels their independence. The Italians did worse. They were defeated by Abyssinian warriors at Adowa in 1896, prompting the Italian government to abandon further expansion in East Africa altogether. In addition, the cost of mounting a military expedition or annexation was expensive. There was a public enquiry in Britain because the Abyssinia campaign of 1868 had cost so much money. Above all, imperial expansion entailed the risk of conflict with other European powers. There was almost a war between Britain and France in 1898 when military detachments confronted each other at Fashoda in the Sudan.

Moral persuasion and sovereignty also deterred expansion
Following the invasion of Egypt in 1882, the British premier Gladstone had no wish to remain in a country where he felt British domination of another sovereign state was morally wrong. However, he would not withdraw until a responsible government had been created and Egypt was financially stable, otherwise Britain might be accused of not having left behind a worthy legacy of sound administration. Many other Europeans shared the reluctance to annex complete sovereign states such as the Ottoman or Chinese Empires. This did not apply to African states such as Zululand or the Fulani Empire.

The causes of imperial rivalry between the European powers

European nations sought Great Power status
Above all, the Europeans were suspicious of any advantage that one power might gain over another and the growth of the British Empire left France and Russia envious and eager to assert their own world influence. When France was defeated in 1871, it looked to new outlets to compensate for its loss of power and prestige. Similarly, Russia's humiliating defeat in the Crimea (1856), and its poor showing in the Russo-Turkish War (1877–78), encouraged its expansion into Central Asia and the Far East. When Germany and Italy were created, they too looked for prestige and colonies, which would denote their Great Power status. There were some who believed that staking out claims across the world's 'empty spaces' (even if they were full of natives) was vital for a country's future survival. Italy, for example, feared that, unless it could accommodate a surplus population (due to a high birth rate), it might face catastrophe in the future. Germany found that, by the 1890s, much of the world had already been carved up, but it still made demands for a 'place in the sun'. Popular support for imperialism, inspired by stories of intrepid explorers, exotic peoples and courageous missionaries, also compelled governments to act.

Despite rivalry and tension, Europeans settled their differences over colonies
The British, Dutch, Portuguese and French had fought wars over colonies in the

seventeenth and eighteenth centuries, but until 1880 penetration of Africa and Asia had not caused any serious disagreement for decades. However, the arrival of new competitors, including King Leopold of Belgium, Germany and Italy, and the exhaustion of available territory increased rivalry and international tension. Nevertheless, the European powers were not prepared to risk wars over relatively valueless territory in Africa and Asia. The overall effect was the worsening of relations, but not conflict.

The European rivalries were extended to Africa and Asia

In 1882, the British occupation of Egypt angered France which thought it had a special relationship with the country (from the days of Napoleon's invasion in 1798). Relations between Britain and France remained bad until 1898. Italy, annoyed by the French occupation of Tunis in 1881, joined the Triple Alliance. Germany was the common threat to Britain and Russia and their interests in Persia. Although they had been rivals, they settled their differences in a Convention in 1907 and divided Persia into two spheres of influence. Germany also tried to support the Boers in South Africa against the British in 1895 and again in 1899. This action, and the construction of a battle fleet that could lead German colonialism, angered the British and pushed them closer to France. The Italian attack on Turkey in 1911–12 also encouraged the Balkan states to take on the Turks too. This led directly to two Balkan Wars in 1912–13 and 1913, causing great instability in the region.

The partition of Africa

Africans played a part in the partition

Africa was divided up between the European powers so rapidly it was called the 'scramble for Africa'. Despite the potential for conflict, the Europeans managed to avoid war between themselves. However, Africans were not passive bystanders in this process. There were already a number of African empires and powerful states alongside nomadic and smaller, tribal communities. Egypt, for example, controlled the Sudan. The Ethiopians claimed jurisdiction over much of central and East Africa, although their control of the region was often illusory. The Sultan of Zanzibar claimed authority over the whole of East Africa as far as the Congo, but this was dependent on his slave trading agents. In southern Africa, the Zulus were the most powerful military state but several branches of their once-united kingdom were distributed across the south. In West Africa, the Tukulor Sultans ruled a vast area, often through their intermediaries, the Fulani chiefdoms. Beyond these political structures, many Africans decided to collaborate with the Europeans, taking up employment or acquiescing in their rule. Others chose to resist in order to defend their old cultures and identity.

European influence was already well established in Africa before 1879

Algeria was a French possession after a long war from 1830–48, and there was a small colony in Senegal. Portugal had abandoned its control of the West African coast after the collapse of the slave trade, but it still retained Mozambique. German traders opened a factory in Cameroon in 1860. However, it was Britain that held the greatest influence over Africa. In North Africa, British financial influence in Egypt was already significant, and on the east coast, Zanzibar was virtually a British protectorate. In West Africa, the British had established Sierra Leone as a colony for freed slaves (its administration was in the hands of West Indians and Africans), whilst the Gold Coast, a strip of Nigeria and Lagos were coastal colonies for trade. In southern Africa, Cape Colony and Natal were firmly under British rule but their attempts to incorporate black Africans into the administration prompted Afrikaners, the descendants of Dutch settlers, to trek northwards and establish their own countries, the Transvaal and Orange Free State, in the interior.

Egypt came under European influence through debt

In the 1850s, the Khedive of Egypt (Pasha Said) used British loans to build railways, reorganise the administration and abandon state ownership of the land. A French company helped with the most spectacular project of all: the construction of the Suez Canal. When the canal was opened in 1869, it cut the journey time to the East dramatically. This was of immediate importance to Britain because of its lucrative trade and extensive possessions in Australasia, China and India. Egypt's economy boomed when the American Civil War cut the cotton exports from the United States. Pasha Said's successor, Ismail, continued with the process of Egyptian modernisation, and borrowed vast sums from European banks. Yet his greedy desire to construct luxurious palaces, and widespread corruption, meant that Egypt went bankrupt in 1875. As Egypt slid into financial chaos, it had decided to sell off its shares in the Suez Canal. The British Prime Minister, Disraeli, purchased the lion's share of them, giving Britain considerable influence over the sea route to the East. In addition, a joint European supervision of Egypt's finances was set up to protect the huge investments that had been made in the country. The *Caisse de la Dette* was dominated by France and Britain as they held the political posts of Minister of Finance and Minister of Public Works. Sudden economies in spending were resented by the corrupt officials and they maintained their incomes by taxing the poor more heavily, whilst blaming 'foreign interference'.

The British took military action against an Egyptian army revolt

When the Europeans suggested that the Sultan (who nominally still controlled Egypt) replace the Khedive in 1881, it sparked an army revolt against foreigners. Colonel Arabi spearheaded the rebellion for constitutional rule (a ruse to give himself more power). The new Khedive, Tewfik, appointed a nationalist government, but he soon called on British and French support because he feared he would be deposed. Anti-European riots broke out in Alexandria and several people were butchered by a mob. As Arabi's troops prepared to resist a British squadron at the port, Admiral Seymour took preventive action and shelled the Egyptian positions. A landing was made to restore order, but the French refused to take part. A full-scale British expedition under the brilliant leadership of General Wolseley then secured the Suez Canal and defeated Arabi's army at Tel el Kebir (September 1882). Britain abandoned the joint control and informed the other powers that it would withdraw once the Khedive's authority had been established, but, in the long term, it hoped to protect British interests and the security of the Suez Canal.

The British occupation of Egypt had far-reaching consequences

Although the French had unilaterally annexed Tunisia in 1881, the British action in Egypt is usually seen as the starting gun for the scramble for Africa. The French were angry at the permanence of the British occupation and wanted to build up their own interests in West Africa. The British were eager to leave behind them just rule and an enlightened government, but until the finances of the country were straightened out, it was hard to see how the country could be abandoned. Sir Evelyn Baring (Lord Cromer), was appointed as Consul-General, diplomatic agent and advisor to the Khedive. He reorganised the Egyptian army and administration, revised the tax system, suppressed corruption and developed industry. In 1885, an attempt to get international supervision of the Suez Canal (to ensure it was kept open by all the powers) failed, although a convention was agreed in 1888. Nevertheless, concerned by Russian designs on Turkey, the British reserved the right to close the Canal in wartime. In 1887, by the Drummond-Wolff Convention, Britain restated its desire to evacuate Egypt if the conditions were right. The continued British control of Egypt made other powers consider having their own colonies. Bismarck supported Britain in Egypt, so long as it agreed to acquiesce with German colonial ambitions in the future.

There was an Islamic rebellion in the Sudan

In 1881, Mohammed Ahmed (the '*Mahdi*') led a rebellion against Egyptian rule as a prelude to the conversion of the world to Islam. Those who resisted were to be killed. In 1883, a small and demoralised Egyptian force under General Hicks was wiped out, and in 1884, the British advised the Egyptian government to evacuate the Sudan. General Gordon was sent to supervise the abandonment of Khartoum, but he stayed and was besieged. A relief force sent to rescue him in 1885 arrived two days too late and the Sudan was left to the *Mahdi*'s tyranny.

Claims were made over the Congo

The Belgian government had no interest in colonies but King Leopold was attracted to the idea of a vast African dominion. He established the International African Association to promote exploration, but instructed explorers to obtain treaties with African chiefs which placed them under Leopold's protection.

Leopold employed Henry Morton Stanley, who crossed the Congo in an epic expedition, in this task. France sent Savorgnan de Brazza to carry out a similar mission with tribes in the northern Congo and claimed a protectorate over the region. The French also stated, in 1884, that if Leopold was unable to defend the Africans under his protection, then they would do so. In June 1884, the Germans also claimed a protectorate over Cameroon based on their trading presence there.

East Africa appeared to be the target of German colonial interests

In 1884, Joseph Thomson of the Royal Geographical Society explored Kenya but Britain made no claims in the area. However, in November of that year, Dr Karl Peters of the German Colonial Society (1882) acquired the signatures of tribal chiefs just a few miles from the coast of East Africa in areas supposedly under the Sultan of Zanzibar. This had come soon after the Germans had proclaimed a protectorate over Togoland in West Africa, and caused some anxiety in Britain. Meanwhile, in 1883, France sent troops and explorers into Madagascar and declared a protectorate over it in 1885.

West Africa and the Berlin Conference changed the situation in Africa

In 1883, the French extended their influence from Senegal and began to penetrate into the upper regions of the Niger. The conflict of interests that was developing in central and western Africa prompted Bismarck to call the Berlin West Africa Conference in November 1884. At first, the Congo was designated a 'free state' based on the principles of free trade, but Leopold's treaties with African chiefs were turned into evidence that Leopold actually ruled the area. Suddenly, signatures of African rulers were the basis and legitimacy of European rule. The Conference thus dictated that Africans were not to be exploited in European interests and that the Niger and Congo were to be freely navigable, but the idea that European claims had to backed by an effective occupation meant that all explorers, mission stations, or trading posts were potentially the pawns in a geo-political power game.

Africa was quickly partitioned after the Berlin Conference

Portugal's claim to the area to the west of Mozambique was not supported because it had no evidence of occupation, but Bismarck announced, at the end of the conference, that Germany had established a protectorate over Tanganyika based on Peters's exploration. These announcements spurred on the Europeans' claims. Tragically, the resolution on the protection of Africans was ignored. Leopold amassed a personal fortune out of a monopoly on ivory and rubber, but the brutalities his men inflicted against Africans were eventually exposed.

West and East Africa were carved up after 1885

To forestall French claims, Britain established a protectorate over the Niger in 1885. France crushed the Mandingo of the Ivory Coast and the King of Dahomey to establish a protectorate in the former and a colony over the domains of the latter. French influence was extended into the interior, giving France a West African empire of 3.75 million square miles (much of which looked impressive on a map, but consisted of desert). The British defeated the Ashanti in 1896 but the French disputed their claim to western Nigeria and a crisis over border delimitation developed in 1897–98. Nigeria was made a British protectorate in 1899. In East Africa, a boundary dispute between Britain and Germany in 1885 was quickly resolved. The British, through a specially formed British East Africa Company, leased a coastal strip from the Sultan of Zanzibar in Kenya and the Germans adopted a similar arrangement in Tanganyika. Zanzibar was then declared a British protectorate in June 1890, and Germany dropped its claims to Uganda in return for the island of Heligoland (north of Germany). Four years later, Britain declared a protectorate over Uganda, and in 1896, Kenya too, came under British control. In 1891, an Anglo-Portuguese agreement settled claims over Nyasaland in Britain's favour. The defeat of Italian forces in Ethiopia in 1896, eventually led to a recognition of the region's independence in 1906 with vague British, French and Italian spheres of influence.

The Sudan and the Fashoda Incident demonstrated British hegemony in Africa

In 1896, the British government was concerned that other powers may try to assert their control over central and eastern Africa, including the headwaters of the Nile. To preserve British hegemony over the Red Sea and Egypt (and therefore protect their trade routes to the East), and to avenge the death of Gordon, the British sent an expeditionary force back up the Nile to Khartoum. The modern army led by general Kitchener made short work of the Islamic forces of the Khalifa (the Mahdi's successor) at the Battle of Omdurman (September 1898). This also deterred Emperor Menelek of the Ethiopians (who had just defeated the Italians at the Battle of Adowa in 1896) from pushing his claim to the upper Nile. However, a French marine detachment under Major Marchand, crossed Africa from Gabon and claimed the Sudan from its base at Khartoum in July 1898. Kitchener confronted the French force and an international crisis developed. However, France knew that it could not defend its position and was unwilling to risk a war with Britain over a worthless stretch of African territory. It was the lowest point in relations between the two countries, but strenuous efforts were made on both sides to improve matters.

Rhodesia was the result of a grand imperial vision

The mining magnate and millionaire, Cecil Rhodes, dreamed of discovering new wealth in the African interior. He also hoped to see the construction of a vast railway, from the Cape to Cairo, which would become a new artery of trade for the development of Africa. Persuading the British government to grant a charter for the formation of a British South Africa Company, Rhodes secured the Rudd mining concession from Chief Lobengula in 1888 and established the colony of Rhodesia in 1895. This prevented German and Portuguese colonies on the east and west coasts from joining, but Rhodes' railway was never built and he did not find the gold and diamonds he sought. Consequently, he turned his attention to the restrictive government of Transvaal.

Britain established its control of South Africa

The discovery of gold in Transvaal led to an influx of European, mainly British workers. This threatened to overwhelm the traditionalist Afrikaner government led by President Paul Kruger. Kruger responded by denying any political rights to the workers and imposed punitive taxation on the mine owners. The wealth of Transvaal grew rapidly and it seemed that the Cape would soon be eclipsed in importance in southern Africa. Rhodes tried to overthrow the Transvaal government in the Jameson Raid with the secret connivance of Joseph Chamberlain, the British Colonial Secretary, but it failed, attracting the derision of the Kaiser (who sent a tactless telegram to Kruger). The British High Commissioner of the Cape, Sir Alfred Milner, feared that the Transvaal would soon attract the support of all the Afrikaners in southern Africa and he set out to overthrow both Boer republics in order to assert British control of the whole region. In 1899–1902, the South African War, or Boer War, ended in British victory, but the Boers had been armed with modern German weapons and Britain was subjected to vitriolic attacks in the European media.

Morocco became the focus of international attention

French designs on Morocco were disputed by Germany, as a pretext, by the Kaiser, for asserting his authority in international affairs. This is dealt with in more detail in Chapter 10.

Imperialism in Asia

Central Asia was the zone where Russian and British interests collided

When, in the 1850s, Russia successfully subdued the tribes of the Caucasus, it turned its attention to the khanates of Central Asia which had once been rich trading cities on the ancient Silk Route. In the 1860s, Russia annexed eastern Turkestan and in 1873, it captured the ancient city of Khiva. Unsure if the Russians intended to press southwards, there was considerable debate in Britain about the policy to be adopted. Liberals tended to favour a peaceful approach to Russia, and the confinement of British interests to the improvement of India. Others argued that Russia would next annex Afghanistan and then threaten India. In 1885, this fear appeared to be confirmed when Russian troops defeated an Afghan outpost in the Penjdeh Incident, and Britain and Russia threatened to go to war. The British and Russians despatched explorers and agents in a shadowy intrigue called 'the Great Game'. Those that favoured a 'forward policy' supported a British invasion of Afghanistan in 1878-80, but the occupation was too expensive to maintain and a client ruler, Abdur Rahman, was installed.

Russia continued to annex territory in Central Asia until the borders of British India and the Tsar's domains were separated by a strip of Afghan territory just twenty miles across.

Russia and Britain were also rivals over Persia and Tibet
Tibet was nominally under Chinese control, but the British had failed to establish diplomatic and commercial ties with the mountain state. When a Russian Buddhist called Dorjieff assisted in negotiating between Lhasa and St Petersburg, the British were anxious that the Russians intended to create a satellite state that would border India. A military mission under Colonel Younghusband occupied Lhasa in 1904 but his actions were quietly disowned by the government. In Persia, rivalry for railway concessions and influence was to some extent resolved by the Anglo-Russian Convention of 1907. Persia was divided into three zones: the north was a Russian sphere of influence, the south was a British sphere and the central belt was neutral. Tibet was to be neutral. However, intrigues continued and the Anglo-Russian Entente was hardly cordial.

China was a weakened empire maintained by the Europeans
The ancient Manchu dynasty had been defeated twice in the nineteenth century by Britain and France. Its old restrictions on trade were removed and China was forced to open its doors to the West, which it despised as alien and barbarian. Nevertheless, under Western influence, China began a painful process of modernisation. Authority was delegated from the imperial court at Beijing to local viceroys and each raised military forces. Customs and ports were reorganised, mines, railways and textiles were developed with European investment. However, this modernisation failed to win over the population. The people became even more resentful of Western influence and felt a deep sense of humiliation.

In contrast to China, Japan's modernisation was a great success
Japan embraced Western methods with enthusiasm after a defeat in 1867. Mutsuhito, the Emperor, abolished the old feudal system and developed a new centralised bureaucracy on Western lines. Industry, education and the sciences were all introduced at great speed. The Japanese were highly disciplined and very industrious, and there was no resistance to change as there was in China. Its new army was styled on the European model and the new navy was trained by the British. When Japan forced its neighbour, Korea, to open treaty ports for trade, China became its chief rival. In 1894, war broke out and the Chinese were soundly defeated. Japan was forced to relinquish control of Port Arthur by Russian pressure (and was furious when the Russians took it for themselves in 1898), but it gained influence over Korea. China was forced to increase the pace of its modernisation which meant more foreign loans. This, in turn, led to greater foreign intervention. In 1900, Chinese war parties were formed with the tacit approval of the government and besieged the foreign legations in Beijing. An

international force crushed the so-called Boxer Rebellion. Therefore, whilst China fell under greater European influence, Japan emerged as a European-style Asian power.

Japan formed an alliance with Britain and went to war with Russia

In January 1902, Japan concluded an alliance with Great Britain. Britain was concerned by the growing naval power of its rivals in the Far East. The Japanese fleet would augment British naval supremacy in the region. Both powers were anxious about Russian intentions. Japan regarded the construction of the Trans-Manchurian Railway as a threat to Korea and believed that Russia would take that province next. A Russian-occupied Korea would be like 'a dagger pointing at the heart of Japan'. Both powers were also concerned about the annexations of Chinese ports. Russia had taken Port Arthur in March 1898, Germany seized the Kiaochow Peninsula in 1897 after the murder of two German missionaries. Germany then acquired a lease of Tsingtao. In April 1898, France took a lease on Kwangchowan Bay. Britain obtained an exclusive sphere of influence over the Yangtse Valley, and leased Wei Hei Wei and Kowloon. Japan already had Formosa, and the Pescadores Islands from its war of 1894-5. The terms of the alliance were that, if at war with a third power, the alliance partner would be neutral. If at war with two powers, the alliance partner would come in and support the other.

The Russo-Japanese War asserted Japan's position in the region

When Russia occupied Manchuria after the Boxer Rebellion, Japan launched a surprise attack in February 1904. Japan quickly fulfilled its aim of defeating Russian forces rapidly, to prevent the full weight of Russian power being brought to bear. However, it was the defeat of the Russian Pacific and Baltic fleets, the latter at Tshushima (8 April 1905), and internal unrest, that forced the Russians to seek peace. Japan was also eager to accept American mediation when it was clear that it would soon run out of resources. By the Treaty of Portsmouth, Manchuria was restored to China, Japan was recognised as the 'paramount power' in Korea. Japan obtained the Liaotung Peninsula and the southern half of Sakhalin Island. The Japanese victory was welcomed in Europe and explained as modern Western dynamism (Japan) against Oriental feudal inertia (Russia). In Asia, the outcome was read differently. An Asian power had defeated a European state. It encouraged Asian nationalists to believe that liberation from European imperial rule was possible.

Indo-China was gradually annexed by France

France had first opened up, then occupied the empire of Annam after a short war in 1860. Traders and missionaries penetrated the territories that had formerly owed their allegiance to China. In 1885, the Chinese temporarily checked the French advance by winning a small victory at Langson, but, despite some disquiet at home, French control gradually reached up to the Chinese border and westwards towards Burma. Unrest continued until Tonkin, as the French called it, was finally pacified in 1896.

South and South-East Asia fell under British rule

India had already fallen under British control before 1870, but the British added a number of smaller territories to its periphery, including Baluchistan in 1877, the provinces on the North-West Frontier (1881–1901), and Burma after a war in 1885–86 (although anti-guerrilla operations continued into the 1890s). King Thibaw of Burma had courted the French as a way of resisting the British, but the annexation of Burma and his exile to India, prevented France from gaining control of all of South-East Asia. The British thus secured control of the Indian Ocean by their territories in East Africa, their base at Aden, the Indian and Burmese coastlines and their colonies in Australasia.

The Pacific Islands were taken over by the Europeans

In the 1880s and 1890s, the Europeans continued to annex the Pacific Islands. Germany acquired the Marshall Islands, the Caroline Islands, the Ladrones Islands and part of Samoa. France held the Marquesas Islands, Tahiti, Society Islands and the Tuamotu Archipelago, as well as New Caledonia and part of the New Hebrides group. Britain controlled the Gilberts, Ocean Islands, Ellice Islands, Santa Cruz, part of the New Hebrides Islands, Tonga, Fiji, the Soloman Islands and Niue. New Zealand obtained jurisdiction of the Cook Islands and Chatham Island whilst Australia acquired Norfolk Island. The United States also annexed Guam, Canton Island, Phoenix, Midway, Tutuila, Tau and the Hawaiian Islands. These yielded little in the way of resources, but gave the Great Powers naval stations for control of the Pacific and Far Eastern waters.

Australasia was an important pillar of the British Empire

Australia had already been traversed and mapped, and its remotest western provinces colonised by 1870, but it remained a continent of separate states until it was federated in 1901. An economic depression in the 1890s and the risk of French and German expansion prompted British and Australian officials to bring the country together. The general rise in prosperity and population gave the British Empire an important prop in the southern oceans, and there was considerable pride in the successful transplanting of a British settlement, or a 'greater Britain'. New Zealand had also been colonised by 1870, but it was not until 1872 that the last of the Maoris Wars was fought and European hegemony established. New Zealand then went from strength to strength through sheep farming and gold discoveries. In the 1890s, it became the first British territory to grant universal suffrage (to both men and women).

The response of the Islamic world

The influence of the Islamic religion stretched from West Africa, through the Middle East, into the sub-continent of India. Yet, each of the states that supported Islam was bitterly divided. There was a vague recognition that the Sultan of Turkey was the leader of the Muslim world, but this was barely acknowledged as having any real significance even in North Africa. The Ottoman Empire had been gradually breaking up for centuries, and Egypt, which was subject to Turkish suzerainty, had fought and defeated Ottoman forces in the 1830s and 1840s. In addition, Persia followed a Shi'ite denomination of Islam, regarded as heresy by the Sunni majority. In every case, Islamic rulers of khanates, chiefdoms and empires regarded their political power as more important than any idea of pan-Islamic solidarity.

The reaction of individual Muslims to Western influence was equally mixed

In Turkey and Egypt, areas that had traditionally been closely tied to the West, modernity was embraced, whilst further East, Muslim clerics often preached against modern influences. In the Sudan, the *Mahdi*'s *Jihad* (holy war) received support within its locality but none from outside. His movement was essentially atavistic and charismatic. On the coast of Persia, and in Baluchistan, the British found communities living in fear of banditry. The Shah of Persia was unable to resist the economic and military power of Russia and Britain. His armies barely controlled the frontiers, corruption was widespread and the infrastructure remained fossilised in the medieval past. His dominions increasingly fell under Russian and British influence. Further East, in Afghanistan and on the North-West Frontier of India, superstitious and lawless peoples paid little attention to central authority, raided their neighbours and occasionally gave vent to a religious ferocity in limited 'holy wars'. One example of this was when rumours of a Muslim Turkish victory over Christian Greeks and British in 1897 (it was false), initiated a series of uncoordinated attacks by 50,000 tribesmen on the British. They were defeated. However, the overwhelming majority of Muslims, like other peoples of the world, participated in European imperialism as workers, soldiers, policemen, political officials and consumers.

Historical controversies

There is strong condemnation of European imperialism

European imperialism was remarkably short-lived. A young African could have lived at the beginning of the European occupation and seen it go in the 1960s. The effect of that occupation is still fiercely debated. Many argue now that Europeans were racist, bullying and exploitative. They turned indigenous industries into reservoirs of resources purely to serve European manufacturing. Thousands died during the conquest, through famines and fighting the colonisers. Worst of all,

Europeans held supremacist views against coloured peoples, which were so pervasive that they convinced the non-Europeans to believe they were not really human beings unless they embraced Western culture and values. Even then, it is said, they were treated like second-class citizens, or worse. However, Tapan Raychaudhuri takes an extremist and misguided line when he states the British in India during the days of empire were 'the Nazis of their time'.

There may have been domestic factors to consider when explaining colonialism
Bernard Porter argued that there might have been a mutual misunderstanding between the British and Bismarck. Bismarck encouraged Britain to acquire colonies hoping it would antagonise France. Gladstone thought that supporting German colonialism would mean Berlin would back British control in Egypt until Britain ended its occupation honourably. Hans-Ulrich Wehler believed Bismarck acquired colonies purely to win over public opinion in Germany. He once stated: 'All this colonial business is a sham. We did it for the elections.' And on another occasion he said: '*My* map of Africa is in Europe' (1888). Bismarck curtailed imperialism when he couldn't get the support of banks and because it could have meant friction with Britain (*Englandhass*).

Empires may have been evidence of modernisation and globalisation
Whilst historians condemn the excesses of imperialism, some are not convinced the European empires were entirely negative. This spasm of expansion was due, in part, a particular point in international relations where the Europeans had reached a balance of power and were seeking an advantage that might mean their survival or demise in the future. In acquiring colonies they sought to establish what they saw as the best of their own societies: the rule of law rather than tyranny, peace rather than war, Christian ethics over the survival of the fittest. They did not always achieve this and there were some who saw colonies as an opportunity for profit, whatever its effect. It is also suggested that Europeans introduced modernisation. These included railways, medicine, faster communications, irrigation, postal services, bureaucracy, shipping, new industries, electricity, clean water and sanitation, scientific education, legal reform and responsible government. These developments may have occurred without European occupation as part of a process of globalisation of technology, but many historians are prepared to acknowledge that European colonialism brought mixed, not exclusively negative, changes to the world.

Tutorial

Progress questions
1. Why was there a 'scramble' for colonies in the late nineteenth century?

2. What was the significance of the Berlin West Africa Conference of 1884–85?

3. What explanations can be given for European policy towards China from the 1890s?

4. How justified is the view that imperialism was on the wane by 1905?

Discussion points
1. Why does European imperialism generate so much controversy?

2. 'Power, profit, civilisation'. Which of these factors was the most important in accounting for the colonial expansion of the Great Powers after 1870?

Practical assignment
Like some of the other aspects of European history, a map is a useful way of learning. It would be a good idea to tackle each section of this chapter with a map to hand and by making your own notes on each region.

Study and revision tips
1. Notice how the question of imperialism made an impact on European relations. Be able to relate how events in China, for example, had an effect on Russia and therefore on the European balance of power. The next chapter will help with this.

2. Beware of the trap of writing about world events. If you are engaged on a European history course, it is important to stick to your topic area. That does not exclude some comparative reasoning of course.

3. Check your understanding of conceptual terms like *realpolitik*, geo-politics, and colonialism. Make use of these in your work.

10

International Relations and the Causes of the First World War, 1870-1914

One-minute summary – The causes of the First World War are amongst the most debated issues of history. Broadly, the topic can be divided into the long-term origins and the short-term causes. The factors that created the right conditions for war were imperial rivalries, an arms race, the network of alliances that carried obligations for powers to go to war, and domestic crises. The actual causes of the war can be narrowed down to instability and change in the Balkans, the aggressive diplomacy of Germany and the assassination of the heir to the Austrian throne by Serb extremists. It is important to remember that, whilst historians tend to rationalise the past into factors and causes, the contemporary decision makers were swayed by popular opinion, wracked by irrational fears and convinced that the survival of their nation state was at stake.

In this chapter you will learn:

▶ how the alliance network and balance of power stood in 1900
▶ the effect of Germany's *Weltpolitik* on the Great Powers
▶ the effect of international crises after 1900
▶ the impact of the arms race, 1906–1914
▶ the instability caused by the Balkan Wars, 1912–1913
▶ how the July Crisis unfolded
▶ responsibilities for the war
▶ controversies surrounding the causes of the First World War.

The alliance network and the balance of power in 1900

In 1900, the nations of Europe appeared to be in an equilibrium of power. The alliance of France and Russia (1894) contained Germany, whilst the Triple Alliance (Germany, Austria-Hungary and Italy, with support from Romania) prevented Russian or French aggression in Alsace-Lorraine or the Balkans. In 1900, Serbia was sympathetic to Austria and none of the small Balkan states appeared to be strong enough to dominate the Balkans alone. Turkey was still a source of instability, but it had recently been prevented from defeating Greece in a dispute over Crete (1897). Britain stood in 'splendid isolation' (according to the Canadian Prime Minister in 1896) of the European alliances, looking instead to its vast Empire and maritime power for its strength. Africa had been partitioned peacefully, even if there had been moments of tension (as at Fashoda), and China seemed to have been divided into spheres of influence without conflict between the Great Powers too.

There were grounds for optimism about the future of Europe

It is easy to assume that, because war broke out in 1914, it was always inevitable. Modern technology was making communication easier and faster, bringing the continent closer together. There were several agencies that represented international co-operation: the Red Cross (1863), the Postal Union (1875), the International Court of the Hague (1899), the International Office of Public Health (1907) and the agreement on International Copyright. Britain, France and the United States agreed not to go to war without reference to a third party, France and Germany agreed on economic spheres of influence in Turkey, and Britain and Germany seemed to be on the verge of an alliance. The Mediterranean powers had already agreed to maintain the *status quo* in their respective regions in 1887 with British support. In 1900, the Europeans, Americans and Japanese all co-operated against Chinese rebels in the Boxer Rebellion.

There were specific areas of tension

National rivalries were present between France and Germany over Alsace-Lorraine, between Austria-Hungary and Russia over the Balkans, and, after 1908, between Serbia and Austria-Hungary over Bosnia. In central and eastern Europe, many nationalities were denied self-determination including the Poles, Czechs and Slavs. There was some rivalry over African and Asian colonies that prevented the settlement of differences between the powers, and the alliances divided Europe into 'two armed camps' which made co-operation difficult. Economic rivalry also developed as 'second industrialising nations' caught up with the initial lead that Britain had built up. A growing faith in military solutions to solve both external and internal problems (militarism) was also threatening the peace.

The alliances could have contributed to a war

The purpose of the alliances was to either prevent a war, or to ensure that a state was protected if a war did occur. The benefit of an alliance was that a less aggressive power could restrain another, as happened in the Algeçiras conference of 1906 and Bosnian Crisis of 1908 (see below). When international crises developed, alliance partners were often thrown closer together. France and Britain drew closer in the face of German threats in 1906 and 1912, whilst Germany grew more dependent on Austria-Hungary which it believed was the only power that would support it in the face of the perceived *Einkreisungspolitik* ('encirclement policy') of the Entente powers (Britain, France and Russia). Above all, the alliances compelled countries to back each other even when their own national interests were not at stake. Hence Germany eventually went to war because it thought Austria was about to be engaged in a war against Russia, and that would mean an attack on Germany by Russia's ally France. Whilst the alliances did not *cause* the First World War, they acted as a catalyst to the events of 1914 and turned a Balkan dispute into a general European conflict.

Militarism may also have contributed to a warlike atmosphere
European leaders were confronted by a range of internal and external problems. Many leaders put their faith in military forces to solve those problems, because armies had a reputation for efficiency, discipline, loyalty, organisation, strength and success. In Germany, there was great national pride in the army. It had unified the country and seemed to be untainted by political shenanigans. In France, the army had attracted a bad press over the Dreyfus Case, but it was still regarded as the only force standing between national liberty and a German invasion. It was the means by which, one day, Alsace and Lorraine would be liberated. It was also seen in a romantic light as the descendant of the armies of Napoleon Bonaparte, which had once dominated Europe. War literature was common, and there was support for social Darwinist theories that national and racial survival in the future depended on a strong military and a vigorous, healthy population forged by war. War itself was seen as a purging force, able to cut away the flabby luxuries of the rich Western bourgeoisie, or the political extremism of the workers in favour of a wholesome and unifying patriotism. Military leaders, newspaper editors, arms manufacturers and those in heavy industry milked the popularity of the armies for personal gain.

Germany's *Weltpolitik*

The Kaiser was an important contributory factor to the outbreak of war
The Kaiser of Germany pursued a personal agenda of trying to be more respected in European affairs. He was eager to make sure Germany was consulted on all important international matters. Secretly harbouring the desire to construct an overseas empire to rival, and eventually replace that of Great Britain, the Kaiser began work on a German battle fleet to augment an already sizeable army. However, the Kaiser's desire to be respected backfired and he was resented as a bullying and pedantic ruler who was trying to interfere in the affairs of other countries. His breaches of protocol angered others. The criticism made the Kaiser less secure and consequently less predictable. He began to fear that at least a third of his countrymen were *Reichsfeinde* (enemies of the state) intent on overthrowing him, and that the Entente powers were planning to encircle and commercially strangle Germany. He believed that threatening other countries would generate loyal nationalist sentiment at home, and deter foreign aggression.

Imperialism contributed to international instability
Whilst the Berlin Conference (1884–85) had marked European co-operation over the partition of Africa, it generated instability in relations between the powers. Italy's disappointment over the French annexation of Tunisia prompted her to join the Triple Alliance in 1883. The Kaiser's support for the Boers against Britain in the South African War (1899–1902) soured relations between the two powers and prompted Britain to seek allies in the Far East. Japanese anger at Russian

expansion in Manchuria and the Liaotung Peninsula (and emboldened by the alliance with Britain in 1902), led to the Russo-Japanese War. The Russian defeat shifted the balance of power in Europe. Russia was, for the time being, neutralised as a force in the Balkans. This made Austria-Hungary feel confident enough to act unilaterally in the Balkans and annex Bosnia in 1908. This, in turn, set Serbia against Austria-Hungary and made the Russians eager to seize any opportunity of opposing its old rival in the Balkans to restore national honour. However, on the other hand, it was the impasse in relations and unwillingness to go to war over colonies that compelled Britain and France to settle their differences over Africa in 1904 and Britain and Russia to end their rivalry over Persia in 1907.

International crises after 1900

The First Moroccan Crisis (1905–06) tested the relations between the powers
France hoped to influence Morocco, an independent state that had once belonged to the Ottoman Empire, in order to improve the security of its North African Empire. When it urged the Sultan of Morocco to make reforms, the Kaiser and his advisors suspected the French were about to annex the territory. As an opportunity to acquire influence and a 'place in the sun', the Kaiser arrived in a yacht and declared that he supported Moroccan independence and an open door trading policy. He hoped that his words would attract the support of Britain and break up the recently concluded Entente Cordiale. Under secret terms in the Entente, Britain had agreed to let France have a free hand in Morocco in return for support for British rule in Egypt. Moreover, Britain was concerned about the Kaiser's gesturing and his naval building programme. The Germans demanded an international conference, hoping to reveal a French take-over conspiracy and thus humiliate France. The French preferred to offer Germany a port in Morocco, but were eventually persuaded to attend a conference at Algeçiras.

The Algeçiras Conference (1906) went against German interests
By the agreement of the conference, Morocco's independence was confirmed. Customs and police administration were to be jointly controlled by the French and Spanish. All countries would be able to fund the Moroccan state bank, but France would contribute the largest share. However, the Kaiser was not satisfied. Russia, Spain, Britain and Italy had all supported France. Only Austria-Hungary supported the Germans. Britain drew closer to France by holding secret military talks. They discussed where the British army would be deployed in the event of a war with Germany. John Morley felt these talks were a mistake because they sent out the wrong signals to France, and took Britain a step closer to a formal alliance (with continental commitments against Germany) with France. The Kaiser was more determined than ever to oppose Britain.

The Bosnian Crisis (1908) embittered Austria-Hungary and Russia

When a revolution broke out in Turkey, Austria-Hungary seized control of Bosnia, an area under Turkish control in the Balkans. This *coup de main* could have meant a war with Russia, but the Austrians knew the Russian army was in a process of reorganising itself after its defeat in the Russo-Japanese War (1904–05). The Austrians also knew that the Turks would be unable to respond. Above all, the annexation of Bosnia meant that Serbia would be unable to enlarge its territory. Bosnia contained a population that included Serbs and the Austrians knew Belgrade would be eager to assert its control of the province. One school of thought in the Habsburg Empire reasoned that Austria must either incorporate all southern Slavs in its Empire, where it could control them, or face a war for survival. The Serbs called for an international conference and got Russian backing. Russia appealed to Britain and France, but Germany offered unequivocal support to Austria, promising military backing if the Austrians went to war. France was eager to avoid a confrontation with Germany when its Russian ally was so weak, and the British wanted to improve relations with Germany, so a note of disapproval was despatched to Austria. Serbians and Russians felt humiliated and were determined to avoid a repeat of this.

There was continuing tension between 1908 and 1911

The Germans and Austrians felt they had won a diplomatic victory over Bosnia. The Kaiser assured himself that his policy was working. The British were more convinced than ever of German designs for European hegemony. The Serbian government began to support extremist nationalist groups that were working towards the overthrow of Austrian rule in Bosnia. The Russians accelerated their military reconstruction. They became the fastest rearming power in Europe. In Morocco, the French annexed Casablanca in 1908 and arrested German deserters from the Foreign Legion. When Germany protested, the matter was referred to The Hague, which upheld the French action.

The Agadir (Second Moroccan) Crisis in 1911 raised the spectre of war

A Berber rebellion against the Sultan of Morocco led to the French occupation of Fez in 1911. Suspecting an immediate annexation, in July Germany sent the gunboat *Panther* to the port of Agadir to 'protect German interests'. The Kaiser might have felt that the French occupation was a foregone conclusion but that compensation may have been offered by France in the Congo, if a show of force was made. A.J.P. Taylor wrote: 'The Germans had no clear idea of what they meant to do when they butted into Morocco – they wished to show that Germany could not be ignored in any major question in the world'. Britain interpreted the German action as warlike. Lloyd George remarked that Britain would not stand by if 'her interests were vitally affected'. Haldane, the War Minister, warned the Kaiser about the feeling in Britain in 1912. Certainly it was unusual to send a warship as an act of diplomacy, so perhaps Taylor was right to suspect that it was a *lack* of clear foreign policy that was causing tension.

The results of the Agadir Crisis were significant

The Germans withdrew their gunboat and, in return for the recognition of a French protectorate over Morocco, they were rewarded with two strips of territory in the Congo. France hoped that Britain would consider a formal alliance but Sir Edward Grey, the Foreign Minister refused, knowing that Parliament would not support a commitment. Instead, secret naval talks were held in 1912. The British agreed to concentrate the Royal Navy in the North Sea and the Channel, whilst the French assumed responsibility for the Mediterranean. Taylor believed Bülow's (the German Chancellor) aims had been: 'to confront France with the possibility of war, cause Delcassé to fall, to break the continuity of aggressive foreign policy, knock the continental dagger out of the hands of Edward VII and the war group in England and simultaneously ensure peace, preserve German honour and improve German prestige.' In fact, Bülow and the Kaiser succeeded only in convincing the other powers of Germany's desire for hegemony or war.

Italy seized Tripoli and demonstrated Turkey's weakness

During the Agadir Crisis, the Italians seized an opportunity to annex Tripoli. They had already reached agreement with Germany (1887), Britain (1890), France (1900) and Russia (1909) that Tripoli would be an Italian sphere of influence, but the dispute over trade restrictions was little more than a pretence for Italy's ambitions. Turkey, the suzerain power in Tripoli, offered to negotiate, but the Italians did not wait and invaded the province. The Treaty of Ouchy (1912) gave Italy Tripoli, Cyrenaica and the Dodacanese islands. More importantly, Turkey's inability to prevent the annexation of one of its territories, coming so soon after the Austrian annexation of Bosnia, demonstrated her weakness. The small Balkan states believed that Turkey could now be finally ejected from Europe and their own ambitions could be realised.

The Arms Race, 1906–1914

There was a naval challenge to Britain's supremacy at sea

Germany already had one of the most formidable armies in Europe, and its reputation was strengthened by its victory over the French in 1870–71, so when it embarked on a substantial naval building programme, the other powers were curious about Germany's motives. A threat is defined as being the combination of 'capability' and 'intent'. In this sense, Europeans were right to be concerned by Germany's actions. Naval Laws were passed in Germany in the 1890s that enabled Admiral Tirpitz to construct a fleet and the Kaiser was delighted that Germany would have the means to acquire colonies and impress, if not overawe, other countries. The German naval programme put Germany on a collision course with Britain. Britain had enjoyed naval supremacy throughout the nineteenth century, and its vast Empire was dependent on control of the sea lanes.

The Royal Navy had been twice the size of any other two navies of the world put together, but in the 1890s this was impossible to maintain as more countries constructed larger fleets. In 1906, the British constructed a new type of battleship, the Dreadnought, which rendered all previous vessels obsolete. The Germans quickly copied the design and launched the *Nassau*, realising this would put them on a level field with Britain. A race developed with Britain just ahead; by 1914, Germany had 13 at sea and Britain had 19.

There were attempts to control the military build-up in Europe

In 1899, the rules of war were more clearly defined at The Hague and in 1907 there was a commitment to ban inhumane weapons such as poison gas and incendiary projectiles. Germany was a signatory to these agreements but violated them in the First World War. The two conferences were called by powers concerned by the rising costs of rearmament: Russia in 1899 and Britain in 1907, but, in their desire to reach a consensus on disarmament, the conferences failed. Separate naval talks between Britain and Germany in 1912, another British attempt to cut the costs of arms, also failed, probably because the Germans were already committed to war at that point. The failure to reach any understanding meant that government looked to their military and naval advisors for security. This gave military men unprecedented influence. General Conrad von Hötzendorf urged the Austrian government to invade Serbia and surprise the southern Slavs. In Germany, Tirpitz opposed any idea of disarmament and he joined his army colleagues in what Riezler (the Chancellor's Secretary) described as *Kriegslüstig* (a desire for war) against Britain, Russia and France. Sir John Fisher in Britain suggested the Royal Navy 'Copenhagen' the German fleet . The German 'Schlieffen' war plan was particularly aggressive. To work, it required the invasion of France even if it had not declared war, and the invasion of neutral Belgium.

Economic influences are disputed as a cause of war

There were four issues, combining the military and economic factors, which are sometimes thought to have caused the war: the industrialisation of Germany after 1870, international finance, the motives of arms manufacturers and the concept of *Lebensraum* (living space). Trade competition was regarded as the prime cause of the war in 1919 because German firms were able to produce goods more cheaply and dump them in markets traditionally held by other countries (such as Britain in South America). This explanation is less convincing now when one considers that trade between Britain and Germany had been increasing before the war, Britain was still able to trade more cheaply because of its 'free trade' policy and Germany was still protectionist. International finance is also sometimes blamed for the war. French loans to autocratic Russia enabled it to survive and pursue an aggressive foreign policy. However, it is unlikely that Russia would have turned into a liberal democracy simply because the West stopped providing it with loans, and Russia went to war for a variety of reasons – including self-defence against possible German and Austrian attack.

Arms manufacturers and *Lebensraum* conspiracy theories are less persuasive

One theory that originated in the years after the war was that the conflict was the result of a conspiracy by arms manufacturers. Weapons and war munitions made them handsome profits, and Krupps (Germany), Schneider and Creusot (France) did make a lot of money from the war. However, the arms manufacturers had no influence over policy making, they made profits anyway and there is no evidence for the conspiracy. Indeed, some private industries were nationalised. Another idea is that Germany was pursuing a policy of *Lebensraum*, a concept normally associated with Hitler. Overpopulation threatened the food supply, and over-production threatened economic ruin, prompting men like Tirpitz to consider the 'risk theory'. The risk of angering other powers was worth it if domestic problems could be prevented, but above all, the colonisation of Eastern Europe might provide Germany with a solution. The evidence for this idea is limited and ignores the short term causes of the war and the Kaiser's changes of policy. It was not concrete plans, but his inconsistency and aggressive gesturing, that made negotiation fruitless in 1914.

The Balkan Wars, 1912–13

The first Balkan War, 1912–13, ended in Turkey's defeat

In 1909, Russia, stung by the humiliation of the Bosnian Crisis, concluded an alliance with Bulgaria in the hope of forming an anti-Austrian grouping in the Balkans. However, in 1912, Greece, Montengro and Serbia joined Bulgaria to form a Balkan League so as to resist Turkey, not Austria. When Italy annexed the Turkish province of Tripoli in 1912, the Balkan League demanded that Turkey make immediate reforms in Macedonia. Even before the Turks responded, Montenegro attacked Turkey and the rest of the Balkan League joined in. Albania and Macedonia revolted, the Turks were defeated and Serbia reached the Adriatic coast. The Great Powers then stepped in and insisted on a conference in London. In May 1913, Britain and Germany worked together on a solution for the Balkans, but Russia and Austria-Hungary clashed on the future shape of Serbia's border. Russia insisted that Serbia should have access to the Adriatic. Austria opposed this, fearing the Serbs would establish a naval base there to threaten her coast. The Great Powers were concerned to preserve their own interests. Russia wanted Bulgaria to the nucleus of an anti-Austrian coalition and a means to acquire the lands of the old Ottoman Empire. Austria was determined to reduce the size and power of Serbia, which it regarded as a threat. Germany was anxious about Turkey's defeat, as it had hoped to construct a lucrative railway from Berlin to Baghdad through Turkish territory.

The Balkans remained unstable and a second war broke out

The Treaty of London (1913) had agreed to create an independent Albania on the Adriatic, Serbia got central Macedonia, Bulgaria took Thrace and access to the Aegean (but was angry that Serbia had central Macedonia which it was not entitled to), and Greece obtained Salonika, southern Macedonia and Crete. Serbia, however, insisted on retaining a strip of territory it had captured during the war but which contained Bulgars. In June 1913, Bulgaria suddenly attacked the Serbs. Greece, Montenegro and Romania joined Serbia, and Turkey used the opportunity to counter-attack Bulgaria to regain lost territory. Austria was eager to support Bulgaria, but Germany restrained her (because Germany was linked to Greece, Turkey and Romania). Turkey was confined to a small area around Adrianople, Bulgaria was reduced in size and Serbia was enlarged. This fostered bitter resentment in Bulgaria, and over-confidence in Serbia. Having defeated the Turkish Empire, the Serbian government felt it could take on and beat the Austrians. Austria was angry at the lack of German support, and Russia equally displeased by the French and British position. Their allies were thus eager to support their partners next time.

Albania remained a source of conflict and Turkey became pro-German

The Greeks refused to evacuate southern Albania after 1913 and an Albanian raid into Serbia led to a Serbian invasion. The Austrians pressured the Serbs to withdraw in October 1913. To get the Greeks to leave, the British suggested compensation for them in the Aegean islands, but this raised the spectre of a Greco-Turkish war in June 1914. In January 1913, the 'Young Turks' had seized power in Constantinople and they invited a German military mission in to assist them. General Liman von Sanders was despatched but British and Russian protests were made. After much dispute, Sanders was appointed a Turkish field marshal and resigned from the German army. However, it was clear to the British and Russians that the Germans were trying to gain greater influence in the Middle East. The Kaiser, German agents told the people of the region, had secretly converted to Islam and was about to raise a Jehad against the infidels. It is unclear if many believed such stories.

The July Crisis

There were new resolutions to solve problems through war in 1914

There is evidence that, by 1914, patience was running out. In February 1914, the Russian Imperial Crown Council convened at St Petersburg and resolved that only a war would allow Russia to realise her 'historic aims'. This suggested that Russia was prepared to go to war with Austria, and therefore Germany too, to finally assume control of the Balkans and acquire the Turkish Straits. In Germany, as early as 1912, there was a War Council meeting attended by the Kaiser and his military and naval chiefs. The Kaiser asked if the armed forces were ready for war, but Tirpitz requested a delay of 18 months before operations commenced. This eighteenth-month period ended in July 1914.

The assassination of Franz Ferdinand initiated an international crisis

On 28 June 1914, the heir to the Austrian throne, Archduke Franz Ferdinand, made a state visit to Bosnia's capital Sarajevo. He was well received as he was an advocate of greater autonomy for Slavs in the Habsburg Empire. However, the date was significant as it was the Serbian national day, the anniversary date of the Battle of Kosovo in 1389 when Serbs had bravely gone down to defeat against the Turks. A Serbian secret society, *Crna Ruka* (The Black Hand), bungled a bomb attack but poor security and a mistake over the route suddenly placed the royal car in front of an assassin called Gavrillo Princip. He shot the Archduke and his wife at point blank range.

Serbia was responsible for the assassination

The immediate question around Europe was: how involved was Serbia in this outrage? Although it was not known at the time, the head of Serbian Intelligence, Colonel Dimitrievich, was also a member of the Black Hand and he had planned the assassination. On 14 June, he had arranged for the Black Hand to cross the border into Bosnia with the connivance of the Serbian Customs. However, the Serbian government advised that the plot be aborted. The leaders of the Black Hand concurred and the colonel was told to abort the mission. However, the agents on the ground, including Princip, refused. Unwilling to appear a traitor, Pashitch, the Serb Prime Minister, took no action. A vague warning was issued to Austria. After the murder, the Austrian Foreign Minister was remarkably calm. He was eager to work with the Russians rather than confront them, and the Hungarian Premier, Count Tisza, was deeply involved in the Magyarisation of Serbs and Slovenes in Hungary and therefore not interested. At that moment, Count Hoyos of Austria was visiting the Kaiser, and the Kaiser's action changed everything.

The Kaiser promised a 'blank cheque' for Austrian action against Serbia

The Kaiser hoped that Austria would take action against Serbia whilst Austria enjoyed international sympathy over the murder. Yet he went further, stating flamboyantly that whatever occurred Germany would give its full support, even 'if matters went to the length of a war between Austria-Hungary and Russia'. This was a blank cheque to Austria. At this point, on 13 July, Baron Weisner, a Serbian investigator, stated that the Serbian government had not been involved in the plot, and had actively tried to prevent it. This raised suspicions in Austria. The next day, the Imperial Council obtained the support of Count Tisza to back a more aggressive policy towards Serbia, providing no territory was taken. On 23 July 1914, the Austrians issued an ultimatum to Serbia. It demanded a reply within 48 hours and the suppression of Pan-Slav propaganda, the dismissal of certain propagandist officials nominated by Austria, the joint suppression of agitation by Serbian and Austrian officials, and an Austrian-led enquiry into Serbian government involvement.

The Serbian response to the ultimatum failed to meet Austrian approval

Russia, France and Britain urged Serbia to adopt a conciliatory stance. Belgrade accepted all of the demands except the last one. Serbia refused to let Austrian officials investigate members of the government for criminal involvement in the murder. Instead, the matter was to be referred to the International Court at The Hague. However, the Serbians were also counting on Russian backing and felt confident they could win this point of sovereignty. Fatefully, before the expiry of the deadline, the Serbians mobilised their army on 25 July. Austria responded by an immediate mobilisation. On 26 July, the British offered to host a conference on the issue, a move supported by Italy and France. Russia preferred to see the matter settled directly with Austria; Germany and Austria refused to consider any conference at all. Sir Edward Grey then sent a telegram to the Kaiser and his government, asking them to persuade Austria to accept the Serbian reply. Bethmann-Hollweg sent this message to Austria but added that the Austrians should ignore the Serbian reply. On 28 July, Austria declared war on Serbia and the next day, Belgrade was shelled. Yet it was the arrival of Austrian troops on the Russian border that now attracted attention.

The Kaiser began to realise he had made a mistake

It was not until the 28 July that the Kaiser saw a copy of the Serbian reply. He realised at once that it was conciliatory in tone and felt it removed 'every cause of war'. Sir Edward Grey urged the Germans again to restrain Austria but to hold Belgrade, if necessary, as a pledge for their demands. The Kaiser agreed and wanted the Austrians to resume negotiations with Russia. On 29 July, the Tsar telegraphed the Kaiser pointing out that the Austrian mobilisation was a threat to Russian interests. The Tsar recommended that the Austro-Serbian dispute be referred to The Hague. Whilst the Tsar considered some sort of partial mobilisation, the German general staff advised the Kaiser that if Russia mobilised first and Germany did not, the German war plan would fail. Moltke, the Chief of Staff, suggested an immediate mobilisation believing any delays lessened Germany's chances. Bethmann-Hollweg asked the British if they would remain neutral if Germany went to war with France and Belgium but took no territory. Britain rejected this idea. Bethmann-Hollweg and the Kaiser then urged Austria to consider the British peace proposal, fearing that a war was imminent. However, at the same time, Moltke telegraphed the Austrian Chief of Staff saying 'Germany with you unconditionally' and advising the Austrians to ignore Britain and mobilise against Russia. The Austrians wondered 'who runs the German government?'

The Russians mobilisation persuaded Germany and Austria-Hungary to act

When the Tsar was informed that partial mobilisation was not possible, he accepted full mobilisation must go ahead on 30 July. Austria responded the next day by announcing full mobilisation measures and Germany declared a 'state of war emergency'. Germany sent a 12-hour ultimatum to Russia demanding her demobilisation. Berlin also asked the French government if it intended to support Russia and the French responded that they would be guided by their own interests. On 1 August 1914, Germany mobilised and, having had no reply from St Petersburg, declared war on Russia. France reacted by mobilising on the same day. Germany's efficient war machine meant that her troops crossed the border of Luxembourg on the 2 August, just 24 hours after mobilisation. The Belgians were asked if German troops might have 'permission' to cross her territory which the Belgians rejected. The next day, the German army was crossing into Belgium. Britain assured France that it would protect the northern coast against German shipping but it was pledged to defend Belgian neutrality by the Treaty of London (1839) and the German violation of its borders brought the British Cabinet together. Germany declared war on France and Belgium on 3 August. The following day, Britain declared war on Germany.

Responsibility for the war

Austria and Russia could be seen as aggressors

After the war, it was widely felt that the Kaiser was personally responsible for the conflict. In the 1920s, the mood changed and many felt that all the Great Powers had shared some responsibility for the disaster. Lloyd George remarked that the powers had 'slid into war'. However, amongst the prime candidates was Austria. It had presented a harsh ultimatum (Grey called it: 'the most formidable document ever presented to an independent state') and its élites thought its problems could only be settled by war. It was the first to start fighting and it had threatened Russia. However, it had the least the gain by a war and thought the fighting would be limited to the Balkans. It was certainly encouraged to act by Germany. Nevertheless, the timing of the ultimatum was carefully planned. It was presented after French diplomats had left the Russian capital, in an attempt to delay the Entente powers' objections. Russia was the first to mobilise (29 July) beyond the immediate arena of dispute and that meant there would be little chance of a settlement. It had strong reasons to act aggressively since it wished to avoid another foreign humiliation (as over Bosnia in 1908) which might also lead to more domestic unrest.

Britain and France had urged a peaceful solution

France played little part in the crisis although it had taken some preparatory military measures as early as 27 July. The French also did little to restrain Russia. However, France supported British peace initiatives and was only engaged once Germany had begun to act militarily against her. Britain, too, was eager to preserve peace. British politicians were more interested in events in Ireland in the summer of 1914 than in south-east Europe. A British newspaper even carried the headline: 'To Hell with Serbia'. The British could be accused of having not made their position clearer to the Germans, but this is unconvincing in light of Grey's efforts for peace. The Kaiser was fully aware that the invasion of Belgium would mean war with Britain, but he regarded the puny British land forces as 'a contemptible little army'. He was to regret the expression many times in the next four years.

Responsibility for the war rests with Germany

In 1919, the victorious Allied powers were right to identify Germany as responsible for the war in their famous 'War Guilt Clause' of the Treaty of Versailles. Germany had the strongest army in Europe yet it did not urge restraint on Austria. It issued a 'blank cheque' to Austria on 5 July and effectively a second one on 29 July. It possessed an aggressive war plan that demanded the invasion of a neutral country, Belgium, and an attack on France, even if the French had not declared war. This was to avoid the scenario of a war on two fronts against France and Russia at the same time. However, this reasoning meant that no war involving Austria and Russia could ever be limited to Eastern Europe, but would immediately engulf the whole continent. To some degree, the Kaiser had blundered into war. The Chancellor Bethmann-Hollweg appeared to be overwhelmed by events. The army seemed to be working to their own agenda. Yet Germany's role in the causes of the war continues to generate controversy.

Controversies surrounding the causes of the First World War

The Marxist view is now seen as too dogmatic and determinist

Marxist historians were always keen to assert that the war was not the responsibility of a particular nation state but a class. The rivalry of imperialist élites, and the extension of competition between capitalist producers into armed struggle was a convenient explanation for the outbreak. The natural result of competition over resources and the concentration of those resources into fewer and fewer hands was bound to result in war, they argued. The Marxists also believed that domestic factors were important. Fear of proletarian revolution meant that the élites sought some distraction in war. These dogmatic explanations failed to take account of many other factors. Political leaders were driven more by nationalist rivalry than by economic or class solidarity when making their decisions. A fear of internal revolution might be more appropriate to explain actions in Russia and Germany, rather than in the Western states, but this does not account for Serbia's ambitions or Austria's calculations after the lull of four weeks between the assassination and the delivery of the ultimatum. Not all of the capitalists benefited from the war, and certainly there is no evidence that they planned it. Some industries were ruined by the war. Most traders and manufacturers could make more money in peacetime. Nor was war inevitable.

There had been a number of occasions before 1914 when fighting had been averted through diplomacy. Non-economic factors were thus as important as economic ones.

Fischer's thesis upset the historiography of Germany and the war

Until 1961, the consensus in Germany was that it had not caused the war. Gerhard Ritter, for example, felt that all the powers had shared the responsibility. However, Fritz Fischer produced a book entitled *Griff Nach der Weltmacht* (Bid for World Power), which showed that Germany had carefully planned its expansion in Europe before the war, being encapsulated in a document drawn up by Bethmann-Hollweg called the September Programme. This outlined how Germany would acquire territory in Russia, annex Belgium and reduce the power of France. There was considerable criticism of Fischer from amongst German historians. Up to that point, Bethmann-Hollweg had been seen as a neutral figure, even as a peacemaker. Moreover, if the idea of colonies in Europe had been advocated before the Great War, it would place Wilhelmine Germany right alongside the aspirations of Hitler, and thus make all Germans in that period little better than proto-Nazis. Fischer's critics argued that the September Programme was drawn up after the outbreak of war, when attitudes would have been more radical. In response, Fischer carried out a further nine years' research to show that the September Programme was rooted in the pre-war period.

The German historians reappraised Germany's position

Hans-Ulrich Wehler followed up Fischer's work by showing how manipulative the Kaiser's régime had been in using nationalism to win over popular support. The oligarchy of élites fought hard to preserve their privileges. Volker Berghahn agreed, illustrating how the development of the German navy was as much to win over a domestic audience as it was to rival the British. More recently, Richard Evans and James Retallack argued that Wilhelmine society was far more complex and the government had less control than Wehler assumed. Perhaps this, in turn, radicalised the decisions of the élites. The most startling work in the last few years is that by John Rohl. He asserted that there has been a deliberate conspiracy of silence amongst German historians and politicians. Attempts to rescue Bethmann-Hollweg's reputation fail to impress him and he put great store on the Kaiser's War Council of 1912. This is clear evidence, he argued, of Germany planning the First World War.

Tutorial

Progress questions

1. How and why did Austria contribute to the growth of international tension before 1914?

2. To what extent was the First World War primarily the result of instability in the Balkans?

3. How far did militarism play a part in causing war?

4. Why did German relations with the rest of Europe go so badly wrong in the years 1900 to 1914?

Discussion points

1. 'An irresponsible lack of direction' or 'cynical planning for war': which best describes the Kaiser's actions before 1914?

2. Was the outbreak of war inevitable, and when did it become so?

Practical assignment

Organise a debate on the causes of the Great War. Try to write notes for the main speakers who will defend the actions of the Central Powers and for those who will support the Entente Powers. What arguments will you use?

Study and revision tips

1. Do not became distracted by a host of dates and details. Most questions on this topic will be concerned with the decision-making of the Great Powers.

2. Try to place the events of the Balkans in their context. Note that the Great Powers acted on their own self-interest. Notice also how the Great Powers lost control of events and the actions of smaller states.

3. A timeline is a useful way of getting to grips with the countdown to war.

4. Make notes on the question of responsibility – this is favoured by examiners.

11

The Great War, 1914-1918

One-minute summary – The First World War was a war of empires but could also be considered a great European civil war. Although there was a strong public expectation of quick victory, many military men knew from the outset that this would be a long war. When the opening battles of 1914 degenerated into trench stalemate on the Western Front, alternatives were sought in the Near East where Britain and her imperial forces could 'knock away the props' of Germany by defeating her allies. However, the 'siege warfare' in France and Belgium continued to cost thousands of lives. France suffered particularly heavy casualties at Verdun. The Germans, disappointed by the failure of their war plan, decided to remain on the defensive in the west and attack in the east. Here the war remained relatively fluid, with the front line shifting across the Austrian and Russian frontiers. Italy joined the war, but made little progress until 1918. Turkey, which had remained on the defensive, lost control of the Near East and Mesopotamia. Russia collapsed in 1917–18. Despite Germany making a titanic effort in 1918, America's entry into the war (which Germany had helped to bring about), tipped the balance in the Allies' favour and victory was secured in November of that year. Huge quantities of men and materials were involved in the war: it was a conflict on an unprecedented scale.

In this chapter you will learn:

▶ the failure to achieve 'quick victories'
▶ the Western Front
▶ the Eastern Front
▶ the other theatres of war
▶ the economic effects of the war
▶ the Allied victory in 1918
▶ revolutions in Germany and Russia
▶ historical interpretations of the First World War.

The failure to achieve 'quick victories'

The German Schlieffen Plan was launched in August 1914

The German high command was fearful of fighting a war on two fronts, with France in the west and her ally, Russia, in the east. Whilst Austria held the south, and token German forces faced the slow build-up of the Russians, the bulk of the German army was to make an enveloping attack on Paris by swinging in a great arc through neutral Belgium. The Kaiser knew that this would inevitably bring

Britain into the war, but he believed the British possessed too small an army to make any difference. The strengths of the armies were as follows: in the west, Germany had 1,485,000 against the French 1,150,000, the Belgians 117,000 and the British 100,000. In the east, Germany had 400,000 alongside the Austrian 1,100,000 against Russian forces of 1,300,000. In the south, Austria fielded 200,000 against the Serbians' 190,000.

The Schlieffen Plan was flawed, and failed

The German war plan failed to achieve its objective for several reasons. German soldiers were soon exhausted by the effort of fighting and marching across France and Belgium. The reliance on lines of communication for ammunition and supplies confined the advance to certain roads, and army corps had to follow separate avenues to avoid congestion. Consequently, the offensive began to slow down and turn to the east of Paris. The German force had been weakened when the Russians mobilised more quickly than expected. When the Germans met stiff resistance from the British, stubborn defensive actions and civilian attacks from the Belgians and aggressive (if costly) thrusts from the French, they lost confidence in the Schlieffen Plan altogether, and they were checked at the battle of the Marne. However, the Germans began to dig in along the river Aisne, and, in order to outflank them, it was necessary for the British and French forces to march north in a 'race to the sea'.

French strategic thinking had put its faith in the all-out attack

The French troops were dressed in a conspicuous uniform of blue and red, and their strategic plan similarly tried to capture the spirit of Napoleonic warfare by emphasising the attack. The French Plan XVII was designed to drive into Alsace and Lorraine, the two territories lost in the Franco-Prussian War, but the attempted envelopment by the Germans to the north soon caused this plan to be abandoned. Unlike the British, who used firepower in defensive positions, the French attempted to send their men forward with the bayonet. This resulted in one million casualties by Christmas 1914.

Lines of trenches extended across Belgium and France

Both sides tried to outflank each other, but lines of trenches marked the consolidation of the troops and soon a network extended 500 km from Switzerland to the English Channel. The British army suffered heavy casualties in the early days: 58,000 died between Mons (August) and the First Battle of Ypres (November 1914). The Germans had also suffered terribly. They called the Battle of Ypres *Kindermord*: massacre of the innocents.

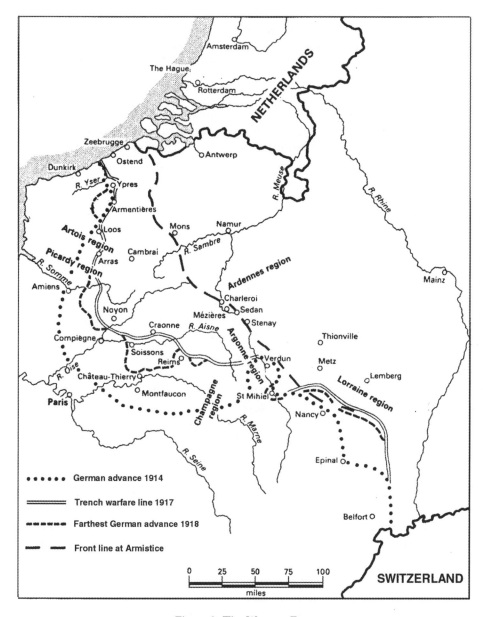

Figure 9. The Western Front

The Western Front

Attempts to break the trench stalemate on the Western Front

In the west, the trench systems continued to develop over a four-year period. Even when objectives were taken, new defences were erected in the rear. By the end of the war, deep belts of barbed wire and successive lines of trenches several miles deep, characterised the front. The Germans, occupying French and Belgian soil, decided to remain on the defensive, elaborating their trenches with deep protective dug-outs. However, to break the stalemate they experimented with poison gas attacks and the use of flamethrowers against emplacements at Ypres in 1915. The British were outraged by this breach of the Hague Conventions of 1899 and 1907.

There was an urgent need for men and munitions in the allied armies

Given the pre-war emphasis on the navy, the British urgently needed more men for its army and it needed munitions. Field Marshal Lord Kitchener, the Secretary of State for War, launched an appeal for men to enlist in the New Armies. The response was overwhelming. In just eight weeks, 761,000 men joined up. Some of these new units were drawn almost exclusively from one area or profession, and the close camaraderie gave rise to the title 'Pals Battalions'. In France, British regulars and Indian Army troops were brought from the Empire to fill the trenches, but there was an urgent need for sandbags, barbed wire, machine guns and, above all, ammunition. France also called upon its colonial forces and it was some of these that faced the first gas attack at Ypres. However, a string of failures through 1915 led to the appointment of Sir Douglas Haig as the new British Commander in Chief. The French were still led by General Joffre.

France suffered heavily at the battle of Verdun

General von Falkenhayn, Chief of the (German) General Staff, conceived a plan to 'bleed France white' by forcing it to commit thousands of troops in defence of the fortress town of Verdun. Reasoning that France would not let the town fall for national prestige, he hoped that the French would deploy men who could be destroyed by artillery fire. The Germans used 1,200 guns to blast the French positions. The French troops were supplied along a single secondary road, the *Voie Sacrée*: 1,700 trucks a day sustained the garrisons. The Germans gradually seized their objectives: including Forts Donaumont, Hill 295 and Fort Vaux. On 24 October, the French counter-attacked and recaptured much of the lost ground. On 18 December, the French had regained their original line. Forty million shells had fallen around Verdun. The French lost 543,000 and the Germans 434,000 men. This made it a battle of attrition, but Falkenhayn had not realised that the Germans would suffer as heavily as the French.

The Battle of the Somme appears to have been a disaster

The British army suffered high casualties on the first day of the battle that was supposed to provide a breakthrough; 57,000 were killed and wounded. The Somme is often seen as synonymous with the blunders of the war. The argument runs that the Somme uplands were poorly chosen for a battle because the Germans had excellent views of the British as they attacked uphill. The second accusation is that Haig's troops were too inexperienced compared with the German soldiers; he perhaps thought that he could pit the enthusiasm of the British volunteer civilians against the machine guns of the German army. The third criticism was his use of artillery. A massive bombardment was supposed to smash the German trenches and barbed wire. Then, at the appointed hour, waves of British soldiers would get up out of their trenches and walk forward, carrying 60lbs of equipment, to occupy the German trenches. In the event, when the British attacked, in many places they were cut down by German machine guns and artillery. Ever since, the enormous casualty figures have been put down to the incompetence of the generals.

Some military historians reject the criticisms of the Somme

However, the battle looks quite different when it is viewed in context. Some military historians have taken a different view from the orthodoxy of criticism. John Terraine demonstrated that Haig's stoicism reflected the Field Marshal's view that the Western Front was one, long continuous engagement requiring the full mobilisation of national resources and some tough decisions. It was not just one battle that mattered. Keith Simpson listed the mitigating factors as: pre-war inexperience of total war, lack of preparation, the problem of adapting to new technology, the strength of the German army, restraints imposed by the coalition partners (France and Russia) and political interference. Paddy Griffith believed that the army's experiences were cumulative and contrasted the inexperience of the early years with the successes and scientific application of artillery in 1917–18, and, of course, the Allies' final victory.

Britain had to support France and Russia in 1916

The painful truth about the Somme was that Britain was obliged to launch an offensive. The German occupied a large slice of Belgium and France, and would not negotiate while it was still strong. Russia was under pressure in the east and France was enduring a massive and costly offensive at Verdun to the south. General Joffre practically begged Haig to launch an attack to divert the Germans from Verdun. Haig was reluctant but the Somme uplands were chalk, where well-drained and drier conditions prevailed, especially in summer. The Somme was also the junction of the French and British armies so that a joint attack here, along a 30-mile front, would double its effect on the Germans. By making a massive attack in 1916, it could double the effect of the Russian 1916 offensive being launched in the east at the same time.

New technology began to make an impact on the war

On 15 September 1916, the first tanks were used and despite the fact they were few in number, they were a remarkable success. Mechanical unreliability and vulnerability to artillery fire were their greatest weaknesses, but they were the greatest technical innovation of the war. They also allowed commanders to retain mobility on the battlefield of the Western Front. New types of poison gas were tried out too. However, the refinement in the use of artillery was becoming apparent and it was clear that gunfire dominated the fighting. New artillery techniques were developed, including a greater density of artillery for the width of the battlefield.

The Germans defended themselves in the west using the Hindenburg Line

In early 1917, the German High Command decided to remain on the defensive in both the eastern and western theatres, in order to break the Italians in the south. To this end the German army retired twenty miles in the west and took up new, prepared positions on the so-called Hindenburg Line. Acres of barbed wire protected concrete bunkers and a five-mile deep defence line.

Nivelle's offensive failed

On 16 April 1917, General Nivelle launched an offensive in the Champagne region on the River Aisne. French troops in the Fifth and Sixth Armies, numbering 1.2 million, supported by the First and Tenth Armies, advanced behind a creeping barrage. Nevertheless, the Germans had prior warning of the attack. They shelled the assault trenches and cut down the human waves in front of concrete strongpoints. The repetition of these attacks, coupled with poor conditions out of the line, eroded the morale of the French *poilus* (soldiers) and mutinies broke out.

The burden of the Western Front shifted towards the British army

With Russia, Italy and France in difficulties by 1917, it was imperative that the British relieve pressure on the other Entente powers. Valuable lessons had been learned from the Somme in 1916. New fuses enabled artillery to destroy wire, the British infantry were better trained, the Royal Artillery dominated the battlefield and infantry-artillery co-ordination had been perfected. In the spring of 1917, the British and Canadians captured the strategic Vimy Ridge and in June, the British and Imperial forces drove the Germans from Messines Ridge. However, bad weather hampered operations around Ypres later that summer.

The Great War became a war of attrition

The chief difficulty with the Third Battle of Ypres (July-November 1917) was that the low lying and marshy ground had been smashed by years of shelling. Added to this was the appalling weather that dogged the attack almost from the start. Some sectors became impassable swamps and trenches filled with water. The infantry continued to attack, but often found it impossible to hold on to ground against German counter-attacks. Tanks foundered in the mud. Wounded men were drowned in shell holes. Even some of the Germans' concrete emplacements slid into the slough, trapping those inside. This battle, more than any other, inspired comments on war's futility from those that endured it, including Wilfred Owen and Siegfried Sassoon. The conditions were not unfamiliar to the soldiers, but the heavy casualties, gas attacks, shelling and exhausting trial of moving in the quagmire of the Ypres Salient marked the battle out as particularly distinct. Estimates of the casualties by the end of the offensive in November vary, but are thought to be in the region of 260,000. The ridges were captured, but the casualty figures suggest that the price was too high to call it a success. The consolation was that the German army had suffered just as heavily and Ludendorff, the German

Commander in Chief, doubted whether the Kaiser's forces could take another blow like Third Ypres. The war had become a struggle of attrition.

Future use of tanks was assured by success at Cambrai

The sign of things to come was the remarkable success at Cambrai. Initially conceived of as a raid, massed tank formations of 476 vehicles captured German lines to a depth of eight miles. A shortage of reserves meant that the ground could not be held for long, but it had proved the worth of the tank. By 1918, British tanks had become far more reliable, and a new light version was being developed. Tanks were also used *en masse*. A herd of 800 tanks spearheaded the attack on the Hindenburg line in 1918 with great success.

The Eastern Front

The Russian invasion of East Prussia in 1914 was badly executed

The German 8th Army was ordered to hold the Russians in the east, but the Austrian forces in Galicia decided not to depend on German co-operation, and advanced into Poland. The Russians were prompted to take offensive action earlier than expected because the French were pleading for a diversion. However, there was little coherence in the Russian offensive, except a vague intention to advance on Berlin and Vienna. Russian troops were also inadequately supplied and their horse-drawn transport was confined to narrow roads. General Pavel Rennenkampf began his attack on the Germans in East Prussia by establishing one army at Gumbinnen and a second army south of the Masurian Lakes. However, the distances between the armies meant that co-ordination and mutual support was impossible. Worse, the commander of Second Army, General Aleksandr Samsonov, was a personal enemy of Rennenkampf. The Battle of Tannenburg that followed on 26-29 August 1914 was a disaster for the Russians. The Russians were enveloped and compelled to surrender *en masse*. Ninety thousand were taken prisoner, 30,000 Russians had become casualties and 500 guns had been captured.

The war in the east remained mobile

The Austrians continued to penetrate Poland (whilst the Germans fought at Tannenburg), but the Russians checked the Austrians near their own border. The huge distances meant that fighting on the eastern front didn't remain as static as in the west. Cavalry and mounted infantry continued to play a key role in reconnaissance, or as screens for troop movements. The Germans, thwarted in the west, decided to switch more troops to the eastern theatre during 1915. The Austrians also managed to crack Russian codes early on which gave them an advantage if they obtained any radio or telephone traffic.

The Balkans theatre also became a stalemate

In the Balkans, the mountain regions were cut by valleys and plains, so the fighting was not as confined as it was on the Italian front. Consequently, Serbia was almost overrun in 1914. To relieve pressure on the Serbians, the allies managed to persuade the Greeks to join the war, but an offensive was reduced to a trench stalemate in the Salonika area. Bulgaria joined the Central Powers in October 1915, as Turkey had done. Thus by 1916, the war had extended in scale but there were no decisive victories.

The other theatres of war

The Gallipoli campaign was designed to 'knock away the props' of Germany

Turkish ships bombarded the Russian ports in the Black Sea prompting Russia, then France and Britain to declare war against the Ottomans on 5 November 1914. However, the Turks closed the Dardanelles straits to all shipping and Russia was soon dependent on the ice-bound ports of Archangel and Vladivostok for supplies. It was hoped that Greece and Bulgaria might join the Entente powers against their old enemies, the Turks. The British decided to send a flotilla of older vessels to force the Dardanelles straits and bombard Constantinople. Mines laid in the narrow channel checked the naval attack, so it was clear that landings would be required to support the Royal Navy from the coast. On 25 April, British troops went ashore at Cape Helles but were unable to penetrate the Turkish defences in the hills above them. Despite major attacks on 6-8 May, a stalemate developed. Fresh landings at Anzac Cove (named after the Australian and New Zealand Army Corps that landed there) and Suvla Bay failed to make any headway. In September, fresh German attacks on Serbia demanded the British switch their effort to Salonika where they could keep open communications. This decision was confirmed when Bulgaria joined the Central Powers in October. In January 1916, the Gallipoli beachheads were abandoned. It was not until 1918 that the Salonika force was able to break out of its position and contribute towards the defeat of Bulgaria. Nevertheless, Turkey was defeated by operations further south.

The Turks were attacked in the Near East and the Middle East

The Indian army was tasked with the protection of oil supplies at Abadan, at the head of the Persian Gulf. Basra was occupied in November 1914 and General Townshend led an expeditionary force up the Tigris, defeating Turkish forces at Kut el Amara and Ctesiphon in 1915. However, outnumbered, he was forced to retire to Kut, which was besieged for five months. The garrison surrendered in April 1916, but most of the 12,000 prisoners of war died in Turkish camps. In 1917, the British recaptured Kut and drove on to Baghdad. British operations tied down Turkish troops and successfully protected vital oil supplies. Further west, a Turkish attacks on the Suez Canal were repulsed in February 1915 and in early 1916. Captain T.E. Lawrence ('of Arabia') worked alongside the Arabs, who had rebelled against Turkish rule in 1916, and captured the port of Aqaba on the Red Sea. In 1917, General Allenby outflanked Turkish defences at Gaza, and on 9 December, he captured Jerusalem. Although delayed by the need to send troops to France, Allenby defeated the Turkish army at Megiddo in September 1918 and the following month, Turkey sued for peace.

The war extended into Africa and Asia

South African troops launched attacks into German South West Africa and captured it in July 1915, despite having to deal with a Boer uprising in December 1914. Togoland had fallen in August 1914, but Kamerun held out until the close of 1915, mainly because of disease amongst the Imperial troops. In German East Africa, Indian troops were repulsed in November 1914, and the war descended into a series of scattered cross-border attacks. In early 1916, General Smuts (formerly a Boer Commando leader) and South African forces drove the German garrison southwards. British-trained East African and West African forces then relieved Smuts' force, and continued to drive the Germans south before pursuing them into Rhodesia. In the Pacific, Japan seized German territories whilst Australian and New Zealand forces took Samoa and some of the German Pacific Islands.

France and Britain persuaded Italy to join the war

Italy joined the war on 23 May 1915 on the allied side in order to reclaim the Irredentist territory of south Tyrol and the Istrian peninsula. The Italians and Austrians found themselves fighting in difficult mountain terrain. There were no less than twelve separate battles of the Isonzo River when the Italians tried desperately to break through. Avalanches, the cold and the altitude added to the burdens of stalemate.

The economic effects of the war

Britain's naval supremacy proved vital in securing final victory

Despite minor actions in 1914 and 1915, when German surface raiders were tracked down and sunk, the only major engagement of the war was the battle of Jutland in January 1916. Although the Royal Navy lost more vessels, the German High Seas Fleet limped back to port and never reappeared. This enabled Britain to maintain a blockade of German North Sea Ports and protect the lifeline to Russia. The German response was to concentrate on U-boat warfare. There was a steady increase in the numbers of British merchant ships being sunk. In April 1917, the worst month of the war, Britain lost 869,000 tons of shipping (373 ships). It was estimated that Britain had barely six weeks' supply of food left in the summer of 1917. The temptation to starve Britain through the total destruction of all merchant ships compelled Germany to announce unrestricted U-boat warfare in January 1917. With evidence of the sinking of the *Lusitania* in 1915, where

12,000 had died (including 128 Americans), the decision brought the USA into the war in February 1917.

The war caused great suffering for civilians

Germany had violated the borders of a neutral country (Belgium) and invaded France. It exploited the industry it found there for its own war effort. News soon filtered back to Britain and France, through thousands of homeless refugees, that the German army treated Belgian and French civilians with high handedness and sometimes with great brutality. In 1915, the sinking of the passenger ship *Lusitania* seemed to indicate that Germany would not respect the protection of non-combatants in war, a fact reinforced by the first Zeppelin raids on London, and by the use of a giant railway gun (Long Max) to shell Paris. Edith Cavell, a British nurse, had been captured in 1915 and was shot, accused of spying. The use of poison gas was regarded as another piece of evidence of German 'frightfulness'. Patriotism was a strong motivation and sustained those not at the front. In Russia, the existing problem of poverty was worsened by a rapid increase in prices and by the misdistribution of food and fuel. In France, food prices increased by 74 per cent by 1917 on the 1914 figures, but wages rose by only 30 per cent.

'Total war' conditions prevailed across Europe

Across Europe, governments imposed censorship to protect public morale, and interned anyone suspected of hostile sympathies. The huge manpower demands meant that conscription was imposed. The governments also directed labour. Conscription was a deathblow to liberalism in Britain, for it ran contrary to the concept of individual liberty and starkly demonstrated state direction. Other European powers had no such problem of principle, but the heavy casualties caused disquiet amongst new recruits and older soldiers alike. Restrictions on food supplies became common, and by 1918 some populations, particularly those in Russia and Germany, faced malnutrition and starvation. In France, the *L'Union Sacrée* was a bond of political parties from right and left, and a new interdependence was discovered when one quarter of the war workers were women. Joffre remarked that: 'if the women in the war factories stopped for twenty minutes, we should lose the war'.

Britain geared its massive industrial potential for 'total war'

The Munitions of War Act brought munitions and armaments factories under government control and banned strikes, lockouts and drunkenness. The ministry David Lloyd George created to deal with shortages was unorthodox. Housed in a hotel outside Parliament, it was staffed with businessmen of 'push and go', rather than civil servants. Despite the claim that it produced startling results, the War Office had already produced a nineteen-fold increase in ammunition in the first six months of the war, but the ministry did continue to drive up shell production throughout the war. When made Prime Minister in 1916, Lloyd George directed that food production be increased, and an additional 3 million acres was cultivated. Wheat production increased by 1 million tons, and potatoes by 1.5 million tons. Rationing was introduced, first for sugar, and later for other products. Bread wasn't rationed but prices on this staple crop were kept down by a state subsidy. At sea, convoys were introduced to protect merchant shipping.

There was growing unrest at war conditions by 1917

In Britain, the trade unions supported the war effort, but a minority on 'red' Clydeside protested against war conditions and ringleaders were arrested. Industrial disputes actually increased during the war, from 532 in 1915 to 1165 in 1918. However, in Russia, disturbances became far more serious. The Tsar took over leadership of the war effort himself in 1915, but continued defeats discredited him. At home, the Tsarina and her mystic advisor Rasputin handled the domestic war economy badly. Strikes, war-weariness and hunger led to a full-scale revolution in February 1917. The Tsar abdicated when his commanders lost faith in his leadership, and the monarchy was replaced by a provisional government. In France, heavy casualties in 1917 caused soldiers to refuse to fight. They marched away from the front or argued that they would only take part in the defence of positions but would not attack. The army restored control by making concessions over leave and conditions, but a handful of agitators were shot. The *Union Sacrée* almost broke up when socialists left the government in September 1917. In Germany, food shortages were beginning to take their toll, and by 1918, bread riots and strikes were affecting many major cities. In Italy, a stinging defeat at Caporetto almost broke the will of the army altogether. The line was stabilised with the assistance of British and French troops.

The German war economy was strained to the limit

The economic aspects of the war were apparent from the outset, and Germany's U-boat campaign was designed to wage an economic war on Britain and France. By the end of the war, Britain had inflicted 24 million Reichsmarks-worth of damage on German industry in bombing raids. In Germany, the drain of manpower in the armed forces affected agriculture: production fell, despite the increased demand, by 50–70 per cent. Germany was the first country to introduce rationing, limiting the consumption of bread, meat, potatoes and fats. Horses were also in demand. In 1914, Germany took control of civilian resources and production with the War Materials Department. Women were enlisted in factory work for munitions and there were increasing controls over information. Censorship and propaganda became essential tools of the war effort. Food shortages eventually eroded German morale, and Austria's army suffered mass desertions when rations gave out in 1918.

The Allied victory of 1918

The German Spring offensive was initially overwhelming but ultimately failed

Having finally defeated Russia in March 1918, the German army swung its main effort at the British on the Somme. A series of sledgehammer blows drove the Third and Fifth Armies back, but Haig managed to hold the line. Unable to break through on the Somme, the Germans tried to break the British Second Army at Ypres. Subsequent attacks were made against the French. Marshal Foch became the supreme Allied Commander to co-ordinate the defence of the Western Front and his priority was to contain the Germans and build up reserves, including American reinforcements. Ludendorff, despite the initial success of his armies, was surprised at the resistance of the British after their initial shock. At this point, the German supply system began to give out, and German troops could no longer rely on captured British depots. Problems in the logistics of the German offensive soon stalled the attack.

The Allies scented victory in the '100 Days' campaign from Amiens

British, French and American forces together maximised the use of tanks, machine guns and artillery co-ordination to achieve considerable success near Amiens. Aircraft dominated the skies, and a rolling barrage in front of the advancing troops repeated a successful formula. On 8 August, eight miles were captured, and Ludendorff knew that the end was coming: he called it 'the black day of the German Army'.

Breaking the Hindenburg Line marked the beginning of the end for Germany

The advance continued and the German Hindenburg Line, a strongly fortified system, was broken in September. The Germans continued to fight, but they were pressed back towards their own borders. Bulgaria surrendered on 29 September 1918, and the Austro-Hungarian Empire fell apart when Czechs, South Slavs and Hungarians unilaterally declared their independence on 31 October. Three days later, the remainder of the Austrian army sued for peace. Germany now faced imminent defeat.

The revolutions in Russia in 1917 and in Germany in 1918

The failure of the Russian army led to the collapse of Russia

In 1916, General Alexei Brusilov launched a well-organised and gigantic offensive against two Austrian armies near Czernowitz. It was so successful that the Germans were forced to divert troops to assist the Austrians. When the Russians reached the Carpathians, exhaustion, lack of supplies and one million casualties halted the attack. Conditions in the Russian army were generally so poor, and food so scarce at home, that the people and the army revolted in February 1917. The army formed *soviets* (councils), and, encouraged by Bolshevik agitators, discipline collapsed. The Provisional Government appointed Brusilov the Chief of Staff, but the failure of his second offensive in 1917 (1–19 July) marked the total collapse of the Russian army. Russia had collapsed because it lacked the industrial capacity to wage a total war and suffered acute shortages.

The Provisional Government failed to solve Russia's problems

Prince Lvov and a group of *duma* officials, augmented with members of left wing parties, initially led the Provisional Government. Although Soviet historians later tried to claim that the workers, soldiers' and sailors' *soviets* were opposed to the provisional government from the outset, there is no evidence of this. Indeed, Alexander Kerensky, who succeeded Lvov, was actually the chairman of the Petrograd *soviet* council. The government became unpopular for a number of reasons. The publication of the war aims, which included territorial annexation, angered the majority of Russians who felt the war was one of self-defence against Germany. One of the first acts of the Provisional government had been to grant liberal freedoms, but this was in stark contrast to western governments who were temporarily suspending civil liberties to safeguard public morale and a united war effort. The government stalled the resolution of the land question, knowing that peasant soldiers would be anxious about missing out on any redistribution of the land, and promises of an election were also delayed (until November 1917). Protesting workers and extremist agitators in Petrograd were shot down in the so-called 'July Days' and Kerensky appeared to side with a right-wing *coup* attempt in September, both of which discredited the Provisional Government.

Communists took over in Russia

Bolshevik revolutionaries seized control of the capital in October 1917, and then set about abolishing all the apparatus of democracy. Making false promises about delivering peace, bread and land to the peasants, the communists secretly hoped for a world revolution, and the nationalisation of land. When opponents started to be arrested and shot, and the elected assembly (of which the communists only won a quarter of the seats) was abolished at gunpoint, a civil war broke out. Millions died, and Bolshevik economic policies (requisitioning to feed the army and the cities called War Communism) caused a famine in which ten million Russians perished. An attempt by the sailors of Kronstadt to reduce Bolshevik authoritarianism was brutally suppressed in 1921 and the secret police carried out a reign of terror.

There had been unity of purpose in Germany at the beginning of the war

When war was declared, the majority of the German population supported it. The Kaiser is alleged to have said, on entering the *Reichstag*, 'I see no parties here: only Germans'. This political unity in 1914 was known as the '*Burgfrieden*', but it did not last the war. When the Schlieffen plan failed to give them victory, German scientists turned to finding new technologies to break the trench deadlock that followed. Gas was used and flamethrowers introduced in 1915. The Germans developed their own tank in response to the British model, but it was inferior and could not cross trenches. New fighter aircraft were built which could fire through propellers to win air supremacy, whilst bombers and Zeppelins were used to disrupt and demoralise the British and French. None of these weapons provided a breakthrough. In 1917 Russian armies began to collapse in revolutionary ferment. In 1918, Hindenburg (the Commander in Chief from 1916) and Ludendorff (the Chief of the Staff) forced the Russians to conclude the Treaty of Brest Litovsk. This gave the Germans control of vital food supplies (in the Ukraine) and industry.

Germany took steps to fight an industrial war
In 1917, Germany was fully geared to total war under the Hindenburg Plan. The army took priority in all matters (transport, food and industrial output). Distribution of all resources came under army control in order to win the war. Conscription was applied to all men between 17 and 61. The Chancellor, Bethmann-Hollweg, promised political reforms after the war to gain support, but he was sacked by his political rivals. However, Chancellors Michaelis and Hertling were weak and Hindenburg effectively ran Germany. The Reichstag passed a resolution calling for peace without annexations in Europe. It was ignored, especially when Russia collapsed, because the high command felt the war could now be won. Some concessions were granted to the trade unions, although they were effectively suspended until the end of the war. In response, groups of fifty workers at a time began to form workers' councils on the Russian *soviet* model. To counter this, Ludendorff launched the Fatherland Party in late 1917 (it was not really a party, but a propaganda effort). One of its initiatives meant that the soldiers of the army were given an educational programme to stress peace through victory. This was effective; the Fatherland Party had more supporters than the SPD at its height.

Germany lacked the industrial capacity to win against the Allies
However, Germany was weak in this industrial war. The Royal Navy blockade reduced its imports of vital war materials. In addition, whereas the total Allied manpower in the war was 40.7 million, the Central Powers' was 25.10 million of which Germany provided 13.25 million. The total expenditure on the war (1913 prices) for the Allies was 57.7 billion dollars, the Central Powers 24.7 billion of which Germany spent 19.9 billion. The combined American, French, and British steel production in 1913 was 44.1 million tonnes. Germany and Austria's was 20.2 million. The total industrial potential (based on an index where Britain in 1900 was 100) was calculated at 472 for the Allies, but only 178 for the Central Powers.

The effects of blockade ensured the final collapse of the German war effort
Germany launched a final all-out offensive in March 1918 against the British army in order to break it and secure the Channel ports. They wanted to win before the Americans arrived in large numbers. The attacks were all contained by

the British and the French, with the American contingents in support. Shortages in Germany caused by the Royal Navy's blockade had reached crisis levels in many cities and food riots were an indication that the war effort could no longer be sustained. There was growing war-weariness amongst the troops too. In the summer of 1918, the Allies launched a series of offensives in the west and rolled the German forces back. Ludendorff brought Social Democrats into the government in an attempt to mollify the Allies. With defeat on the battlefields of France and Flanders, the Germans first called for peace on the basis of the Fourteen Points (which the Americans had put forward, but which the Germans had rejected), and then accepted an Armistice on 11 November 1918. This was due in part to the outbreak of a mutiny in the German navy at Kiel on 20 October 1918. Amid revolutionary chaos in Germany, and a declaration of a republic by the Social Democrats on 9 November, the Kaiser abdicated and fled to Holland.

Historical interpretations of the First World War

The war had been the most costly in Europe's history

The Hundred Days and the German capitulation in November 1918 indicate that the Allies had won the Great War, but after the war, the scale of the losses gave rise to a determination never to go to war again. Three quarters of a million British and Empire soldiers, sailors and airmen died on the Western Front. Britain itself lost a total of 650,000 with 1.6 million permanently disabled. Germany lost 1.8 million, France 1.3 million, Russia 1.7 million, Austria-Hungary 1.2 million and Italy 460,000. For a long time, it was thought that the 'flower' of European youth had perished: the best, brightest and fittest. This was probably because the junior officer corps, drawn from the educated middle classes and aristocracy, had suffered proportionally higher casualties. However, the terrible losses amongst the battalions of Europe's armies, devastated small communities. Thousands of families lost a family member. Death did not respect rank or status, the great and the humble lost sons, brothers, and friends. Towards the end of the war, and for several months after, an epidemic of Spanish influenza killed thousands of people already weakened by malnutrition and hardship. Yet there was little sympathy for the Germans in 1918. An army of occupation stood on the Rhine and the allies demanded that Germany pay for the damage and sorrow it had inflicted on the rest of the world. Sadly, this nurtured a desire for revenge in the hearts of German nationalists that would lead to another, even more costly world war.

The war ended several of the old empires that had dominated Europe

The Brusilov Offensive, A.J.P. Taylor once noted, 'marked the moment when the armies of Austria-Hungary lost their fighting spirit' and he claimed that it was only Germany that kept them in the war. Yet this one offensive also marked the last gasp of the Romanov dynasty. Its failure and the massive casualty toll mobilised thousands of Russians to protest and the Tsar abdicated. His successor,

Duke Michael, simply refused to replace him and the régime collapsed. The Turkish Empire proved more resilient, but its armies were sustained by a deep Islamic faith. The Turks were engaged in a holy war. Nevertheless, the Arabs had had enough and readily shook off their former masters. Expecting full independence, there was widespread anger when British and French Mandates, offered by the League of Nations, meant the establishment of European control in place of Turkey's. When Arthur Balfour declared in 1917 that the Allies would endeavour to permit Jewish immigration (as a move to win over the Jewish lobby in America), Arabs felt a sense of betrayal. However, it was the fall of the German Empire that was to have the most significant ramifications. The failure of the 1918 offensive, in the words of A.J.P. Taylor, 'shattered their faith in victory ... they no longer wanted to win. They wanted only to end the war'. However, they did not secure the honourable peace they had hoped for. Deprived of territory, substantial armed forces, colonies and money, the German right wing harboured a wounded resentment of the Allies.

Tutorial

Progress questions
1. Why was it impossible for any power to achieve a quick victory in 1914?

2. What methods did the armies try to use to break the deadlock of the Western Front?

3. How far was the war the cause of a revolution in Russia?

4. Why did the Germans lose the First World War?

Discussion points
1. Were the generals of the European armies in the First World War incompetent?

2. Why did civilians become the target of European armed forces, and subject to governments' propaganda efforts?

Practical assignment
Using a map, locate the fronts of the First World War. Annotate onto this map the major developments of 1914–1918. Can a turning point in the war be identified? Why did the war spread as it did across so many parts of Europe and the world?

Study and revision tips
1. Notice how the war brought to an end the Empires of Russia, Austria and Germany. Be prepared to account for these events.

2. The role of governments and the attitudes of the domestic populations were as important as the various military aspects of the war. You should be able to

write about these points and that requires some careful preparation. Add these notes to your study of each country.

3. The European Empires were drawn into the war, making it a global conflict even before the USA declared war in 1917. This fact should be used to fully evaluate the purpose of the empires for contemporaries in this period.

12

Historical Concepts and Conclusions

One-minute summary – Good quality historical writing requires a clear use of concepts and an ability to analyse broad trends and developments. It is very easy to be drawn into the detail, and 'fail to see the wood for the trees'. This chapter summarises the most important concepts and tries to link together the themes of European history in outline. Essentially this period can be seen as the 'Rise of the West' to global pre-eminence. In the space of three decades, Europeans (and their descendants from earlier colonial periods) had taken control of the rest of the world. The Western economy (which includes the United States) became the dominant system, and European values and ideas were transmitted across the continents. However, within Europe, international rivalry became more acute, and each country faced unrest from its own work forces or minorities. Extreme solutions were proposed and an ideological divide of conservativism against revolutionary socialism emerged, with moderate democrats caught between them. These impulses could not be contained so that, when war broke out, it was greeted with a sense of relief. It was hoped that, like some oppressively thundery day, the storm would clear the air. In fact, the war swept away all the old assumptions in Europe, and created its own bitter problems for the future. The world would never be the same again.

In this chapter you will learn:

- ▶ about concepts common throughout European history
- ▶ conclusions on the rise of the West
- ▶ changes in the European economy
- ▶ changes in European society
- ▶ changes in political ideas
- ▶ international diplomacy
- ▶ the impact of war on this period of history
- ▶ European integration and disintegration.

Concepts in European history

Liberalism was a concept that favoured gradual and peaceful change

The American and French Revolutions at the end of the eighteenth century had promoted the idea of individual and collective liberty against tyranny. By the mid-nineteenth century, European liberals embraced the notion that societies could be changed to benefit the greatest number by a gradual and peaceful process of evolution. The aim of this process was to preserve and promote individual liberty, but it was to be in a moderate form. The liberty of one person should not, it was argued, infringe on the liberty of another. Individuals should have freedom of expression, of speech, of conscience, of assembly and the right to possess property. There should be respect for the law, and citizens should conduct themselves peacefully. Liberals also favoured the idea that free exchange, or 'free trade', would bring mutual benefit to individuals and to nations. Monarchies could be tolerated but only if the head of state was limited by a constitution. In the western European states, democratic liberal movements were already well established in power. In central and eastern Europe, democrats were still suppressed and sometimes persecuted.

Conservatism was fighting a rearguard action
In Britain, Conservatives were essentially democrats who wished to preserve the *status quo* of limited monarchy but also a limited franchise. They opposed too much reform as disruptive and a dangerous encouragement to ill-educated and ill-disciplined mob rule. They aimed to uphold the Empire, the Protestant denomination and the monarchy. In central and eastern Europe, conservatives did not have to contend with a democratic system. Conservatives were an élite of landowners, industrialists or wealthy noblemen who wanted to prevent the growth of democracy and so preserve their hold on power and privilege. They were prepared to pander to democratic ideas and demagoguery in order to win over the masses, but they favoured their religion, élitism and feudal authority over any real power-sharing. In an era of rapid industrialisation, population growth, and the development of a mass media, hanging on to power was increasingly difficult. More radical right-wing solutions were suggested, including war and the forced suppression of democratic ideas.

Nationalism and militarism were common throughout Europe
In the early nineteenth century, it was apparent that a common political consciousness was emerging amongst the broad mass of the people of Europe based on their nation states. Nationalism bound peoples together under a shared identity, often based on language and culture, place or history. In many cases this identity was defined by reference to others as different, as sometimes even as either inferior or superior. Nationalism was thus distinct from patriotism (a sentiment of belonging and respect for institutions and laws) in that it promoted race, custom, and language in a supremacist and belligerent way. Nationalism allowed individuals to subsume their responsibilities in a shared mission. This was not dissimilar from militarism: a passion for all things military. The martial values of self-sacrifice, courage, efficiency, organisation, precision, and masculinity were appealing to peoples who wanted to believe that their nations were the best.

Social Darwinism and racialism were considered in intellectual circles
Social Darwinism applied the principles first expounded by Charles Darwin on the animal kingdom to the human race and to nation states. Although few

Europeans fully subscribed to the idea, many were influenced by it through literature and the media. The rise and fall of empires were more evident to the Europeans in the late nineteenth century than ever before, as large parts of Africa and Asia fell under European control. It was felt that some nations, owing to the races that constituted them, were stronger than others. In the fierce competition of international diplomacy, imperialism, capitalism and war, some nations, like animal species, would not survive. Only those peoples who were racially fit (with the right physical attributes as well as mental robustness or 'character') would survive. There was widespread concern when any evidence of 'degeneracy' was discovered, a fact that prompted many investigations into mental health and the state of the urban and rural poor. Europeans also categorised the non-European world into racial stereotypes. The fittest races were sometimes incorporated into imperial administration and military forces, but others were condemned as incapable of improvement. Jews, gypsies and some racial minorities in Europe itself were also categorised as inferior and were persecuted.

Imperialism was an extension of European politics

Imperialism is the extension of power through conquest and dominion. Empires existed long before the nineteenth century and beyond Europe, but the Portuguese, Spanish and Dutch empires of the sixteenth centuries had become moribund. France had lost many of its colonies to Britain in the eighteenth century. Disraeli promoted the idea of empire as Britain's means to enhancing its Great Power status, especially in the eyes of its own population. Others saw empire as a means to promote European values: the care of Christianity, the improvements of commerce and the advancement of modern civilisation. Joseph Chamberlain, the Colonial Secretary of the 1890s, believed that in the future the world would be dominated by super states which would included Russia and America, and, if it developed an empire, Great Britain too. When France and Germany began to acquire more colonies in Africa, Chamberlain felt the empire should be an economic zone bonded together by free trade principles and mutual military support. J.A. Hobson offered a different analysis, thinking imperialism little more than a conspiracy of financiers to invest their money overseas rather than spend it on improving the lot of the labouring classes. Lenin agreed in his critique of 1916, suggesting that capitalist societies were about to collapse and imperialism was evidence of their desperate search for new areas of investment in the end game of competition. Hobson and Lenin were wrong. It was a phenomenon driven as much by Great Power rivalry, the desire for prestige, military operations on the periphery of older bridgeheads and the efforts of traders, planters, missionaries and administrators. Yet it produced a significant legacy and the world is still coming to terms with the European colonial experience.

Marxism and socialism were influential in popular politics
Karl Marx (1818–1883) was a German intellectual who argued that all history was a continuous struggle between classes for supremacy. His influential *Communist Manifesto* (1848) called on workers of the world to unite and throw off their oppressive capitalist overlords. The message reached few workers at first, but caught the attention of many European radical thinkers who already favoured the principles of socialism. In fact a deep rift gradually developed between those who subscribed to Marx's ideas of change through a violent revolution and those who preferred to work with existing élites to bring about gradual change through reform. Bitter debates were evident between the German gradualists led by Eduard Bernstein and the Marxists led by Karl Kautsky, Rosa Luxembourg and Karl Leibknecht. Amongst Russian intellectuals, Lenin's Bolsheviks demanded revolution through a specially trained élite, but the traditional left still favoured a Russian-style revolt through the peasantry or anarchic action through assassination and terrorism.

Conclusions: the rise of the West

The most striking phenomenon of the period 1870–1914 is the development of the capitalist economy of Europe. This had consequences that were not confined to Europe, but which were global. Cheap goods could be manufactured on an unprecedented scale and at great speed, cutting the costs of production. This made products and food available to Europeans in abundance, freeing the population from a life of subsistence agriculture and permitting specialism in technical trades, research, engineering and science. Steam power assisted in the acceleration of transport, greater efficiency in the extraction of minerals, and greater flexibility at sea. The Europeans were the most organised and advanced civilisation in the world. These advances enabled Europeans to dominate the rest of world militarily, commercially and financially.

Changes in the European economy

There were many inventions in communications at the end of the nineteenth century
Joseph Mornier of France introduced steel reinforced concrete in 1867 and it was quickly adopted for the construction of buildings and roads. Alexander Graham Bell invented the telephone in 1876, along with loudspeakers and microphones, which greatly influenced communications. Photography, which had begun in France in 1826, had become an affordable hobby for thousands of Europeans by the 1890s. The first moving images were pioneered by Louis Aimé Augustin in New York in 1885 and the first film performance was in Paris in 1895 courtesy of the Lumière brothers. In 1877, the American Thomas Edison had invented the phonograph to record audible messages. Emile Berliner perfected the idea in 1887

by introducing the gramophone disc. The bicycle became a popular mode of transport and was especially liberating for women who no longer had to put up with a chaperone. In 1885, Gottfried Daimler invented the petrol-driven motor car which gave the rich greater mobility. In communications and transport, the most dramatic development was the invention of powered flight and the successful flight of the Wright brothers in America. In 1908, Louis Bleriot built a monoplane that set the standard pattern of design until the invention of the jet aircraft.

There was a range of new inventions in manufacturing

In 1895 the establishment of commercial plantations in Malaya by H.N. Ridley introduced rubber manufacturing. This was stimulated by the development of motor vehicles after 1905. The first motorcar workshops began in France in 1890, producing one car at a time. In 1903, Henry Ford began a factory for cars in America and by 1913 he had perfected a production line that used standard, mass-produced parts. This concept was to be used to regulate the working practices of labourers but also to mass-produce goods, and later, munitions, more rapidly. Thousands of smaller electrical devices also appeared in this period including: the iron (1882), kettle (1891), toaster (1893), hairdryer and heater (1899), washing machine (1907), dishwasher (1914), mower (1916) and electric clock (1918). Other domestic gadgets included the safety razor (1901) and lipstick (1915).

There were new discoveries in medicine and science

Joseph Lister was the first surgeon to use antiseptic in his work in 1867 and Abraham Groves introduced the practice of sterilising surgical instruments and wearing rubber gloves in operations. In 1895, Wilhelm Rontgen discovered X-rays (high frequency electromagnetic radiation) while working on a cathode ray tube. Their ability to pass through some solid materials and not others, and the fact that they could be recorded on a photographic plate, was a breakthrough for medicine in that bones could be examined inside the body. In 1905, Albert Einstein published his *Special Theory of Relativity* which, by dwelling on space, light, matter and time, offered a glimpse of the structure and nature of the universe. It was one of the most influential ideas in physics and was reinforced in his *General Theory of Relativity* in 1915.

Changes in European society

Perhaps the key issue for millions of working-class people in Europe was how to express their misery and dissatisfaction with their living and working conditions. Greater industrialisation and urbanisation had begun to break up the old deferential codes of behaviour that had lasted for centuries. Crowded into poor accommodation, working long hours for low wages, the workforces of Europe had a tough struggle for survival. Even the skilled and better-off artisans saw their trades eroded and abandoned by the introduction of factories and machines. In Britain, an attempt to revive the old skills in the arts and crafts movement was a brave gesture but the trend was towards mass production rather than quality. From 1867, the propertied working class in Britain had the vote alongside the middle and upper classes. This compelled the politicians of Britain to pay closer attention to the grievances of the workers, and, following a struggle between the House of Lords and the elected House of Commons, the aristocracy lost their influence on power for good. It was not this way on the continent. Denied a vote and a voice, some turned to violence as a path to liberty. Others accepted their lot with resignation. The mass of the rural population, still the majority in eastern Europe, remained loyal to their rulers.

Changes in political ideas

The middle classes of Europe, the greatest beneficiaries of the new industrial wealth, had aspirations to convert their wealth into a political voice. In some cases, they sided with the existing élites against the lower orders. Others looked for greater liberty throughout society led by the bourgeoisie. By the outbreak of the First World War, an ideological divide was developing between those who favoured conservatism and preservation of the existing order and those who sought change through greater democratisation. The means to achieve these ends further divided these two schools of thought. Moderation, concession, and evolution were the options for the peaceful. Others saw the future only through war, terrorism or bloody revolution. On the extremes of the left and right wings, the more radical and violent solutions were dominant. Tired by the lack of progress and impatient for change when the world was developing so rapidly around them, revolutionaries wanted to achieve their aims as soon as possible. The right felt that time was running out. Unless action was taken soon, the mobs would rise up and butcher the élites. Thus, at a time when democratic movements were springing up and some governments were making progress on social and political reform, in the shadows, the extremists were already plotting their violent solutions.

International diplomacy

In 1870–71, Germany and Italy were new countries in Europe. Their presence altered the old balance of power on the continent. Equally the defeat of France in 1871, and then Russia in the Far East in 1905, had important consequences for the equilibrium between the European states. Imperialism had offered the Europeans a chance to enhance their power position with new resources, prestige and colonial allies, but there was universal dissatisfaction with the results. Europe continued to turn in on itself and the diplomats seemed powerless in the face of the passions of nationalism. International diplomacy was supposed to be a part of greater interconnectedness in the world. Free trade had once seemed to be the hope of preserving world peace on the basis of mutual gain and co-operation. International finance also held out the hope of greater integration. However, tariff wars, aggressive commercial competition and fears about strategic weaknesses eroded the willingness of the powers to work together. A complex network of alliances dominated the continent and an arms race fostered suspicion. By 1914, the two armed camps were beginning to put their faith in military solutions rather than an international order.

The impact of war

The First World War was cataclysmic
The 'Great War for Civilisation' of 1914–18, as it was known to contemporaries, was a disaster for Europe. Sixteen million people perished. Large parts of France, Belgium, Poland, Russia, and the Balkans were devastated. Millions were made homeless. Russia collapsed into civil war and fell under a brutal Bolshevik régime. Famine in Russia cost the lives of a further 10 million between 1918 and 1921. In Armenia during the war, the Christian population was uprooted by the Turks and marched into the deserts of Mesopotamia. Between 500,000 and 1 million were killed, or died of exposure and disease in 1915. It was the first planned genocide of the twentieth century.

Wars had been prominent in European history between 1870 and 1914
Until the 'total war' experience of the Great War, Europeans had been used to war. Germany was unified by war, as was Italy. All the Europeans had successfully acquired empires by war and the Balkan Wars, as late as 1913, had been concluded so rapidly it appeared that wars offered quick solutions to difficult political problems. However, it should be noted that the European powers expected the 1914 crisis to be a localised conflict, and not a war that would engulf the globe.

European integration and disintegration

Europe was divided
Europe's nation states were unified on the basis of nationality in the period 1870–1918. Serbia and the southern Slavs had sought to bring together their countrymen in one state, an aspiration shared by Czechs, Croats, Poles and many other groups. The Great Powers defended their interests on the basis of the preservation of their nation state. Alliances, whilst appearing to be a form of integration, were all based on national self-interest. At best, there were some aspects of co-operation such as the recognition of the International Court at The

Hague, but Europeans refused to consider anything but a separate sovereignty. The period between 1914 and 1945 is now sometimes referred to as the European 'Thirty Years War' (emulating the conflict of 1618–48), or even a civil war. During that period, and after, Europeans have remained divided, fiercely loyal to their region and national identity.

Europeans respect and celebrate diversity

Moves since 1951 to integrate and even unite Europe seemed doomed to failure because of the lack of any common historical root (which even regions like Italy and Germany enjoyed before their unification). Yet this is not a cause for despair. Europe's great strength lies in its rich diversity and independent vitality. Its separate histories, each one fascinating in itself, offer an opportunity to understand why the Europeans continue to want to retain their own unique identities. Europeans proved that they rejected authority that gave them no voice and embraced a national identity that offered hope for the future. The Great War proved that any misunderstanding was fatal to the continent. Each anniversary of that conflict should remind us to respect and understand our separateness. We should also celebrate that feeling of '*Vive la Difference!*'

Tutorial

Progress questions

1. Why can the period 1870–1914 be described as the 'rise of the West'?

2. Why did some Europeans turn to extremism before 1914?

3. Account for the changes in European ideas and society before 1914.

4. What explanations can be offered for the divisions in European society?

Discussion point

How united is Europe, compared with its history between 1870 and 1918?

Practical assignment

Try to construct an essay plan, or practice writing an essay in one hour, on the question: 'Despite its problems, Europe between 1870–1918 was able to evolve and achieve world hegemony'. Do you agree? Consider economic, military and intellectual aspects of this topic.

Study and revision tips

1. Construct a timeline for each of the topics in this book to get a general overview of the whole period.

2. Plan your wider reading of this subject. Examiners and tutors will be more impressed if you are able to show an awareness of a number of different authors and sources.

3. Take care always to offer an argument, show you understand and can refute the alternatives and, above all, evaluate the material. Be able to explain why certain events took place and why decision makers behaved the way they did. This will ensure your answers do not become too narrative.

4. Always support each of your points with evidence. One or two examples will be sufficient if you are working under timed conditions. Avoid a list of facts: always weave the evidence into your arguments.

5. Try to learn a selection of choice quotes and statistics. These will add 'authority' to the style of your answers.

6. Get a good grasp of the concepts. Try to use them in your answer, but do not labour a definition – the examiner will be fully aware what the term means but wants to see how you make use of it.

Appendix: Model Answers

'Between 1866–1904, the rulers of the Russian Empire were required to deal with insoluble problems, including those of governing so many non-Russians'. Assess the validity of this statement.

About the question

Note the dates. The examiners will not want anything from outside these dates so you cannot include the 1905 revolution or Stolypin (1906–1911). Tackle each of the elements of the question in turn.

Insoluble problems? This is debatable. You are being invited to challenge the idea that they were insoluble. You should focus on land, the conditions in the cities and perhaps the absence of political reform. One of the insoluble problems for the régime was the threat of revolt or even revolution, and perhaps the rise of terrorist or revolutionary organisations.

Including so many non-Russians? Examiners want you to include these. Some nationalities appear to have given the régime few problems. The Caucasus and the Far East, for example. However, the Poles, the Finns, the Baltic peoples, and Jews (if they can be considered non-Russian which is also debatable) did feature in the Tsars' agendas.

Tackling the question:

Introduction. Do not try to introduce the period. Don't start with some sweeping statement about Russian history. Instead introduce your argument. The best way to start would be to point out what you have just picked out from the question and frame it within your plan. The **main argument** should be that *the Tsars were determined to maintain the system of autocracy. Their main fear was the threat of insurrection. All their measures were designed to deal with this rather than genuinely assisting with modernisation.*

The main part. Make a series of six headings which will be the basis of the six paragraphs you will write in this essay.

Alexander II's reforms were insincere in that they were designed to strengthen the régime. Alexander's conciliatory policy in Poland was to create a greater sense of loyalty. This was also true of Finland. In Central Asia, local people were exempt from conscription to try to ameliorate their loss of freedom in the conquests of 1864–81. His land reforms were only to 'prevent the abolition of serfdom from below' (revolution). Whilst the *zemstva* were regarded by Hugh Seton-Watson as the organ for a genuine freedom of speech, the Tsars ensured the nobility enjoyed a disproportionate amount of control, and they maintained a secret police to deal with any one who was outspoken. This meant that *zemstva* were little more than agencies for the Tsars to listen to the people's grievances.

Alexander III continued the repression Alexander II had already begun. The assassination of 1881 gave the repression greater legitimacy. You should include Russification and persecution of the Jews. You can discuss the non-Russians by making reference to the Finns and the Poles.

The paragraph on Nicholas II should include how unsuitable he was as a ruler who inherited the repressive system of autocracy. You should include statistics of peasant unrest and examples of, and the growth of, revolutionary groups. As far as foreign minorities are concerned, there was unrest in Central Asia (1898, Tashkent), and the revocation of the Finnish constitution. The lack of progress in reform clearly added to the frustrations of the Poles (such as the absence of religious toleration for Catholics). Nicholas continued to promote the conversion to Orthodox Christianity of non-Russians begun by Alexander III (Lutheran Balts, Polish Catholics and Muslims from Central Asia). The army prevented any more than 25 per cent of a unit being drawn from non-Russian stock. Universities were forced to use the Russian language.

Another paragraph might focus on education. The lack of education for the people of Russia reflected the Tsars' belief that this would simply make them ambitious for power-sharing, or revolutionary.

The fundamental point was that Russia was economically weak. You should discuss how Alexander II's reforms failed to solve the country's reliance on agriculture. Alexander III appears to have wanted to keep peasants on the land in the belief they would be more loyal. Townspeople might be revolutionary as they were not as deferential, nor subject to the influence of the church to the same extent. Under Nicholas, there was at least tolerance for Sergei Witte's plan to modernise and develop Russian industry, but this was only to ensure greater prosperity and therefore the contentment of the people. As soon as fears grew that industrialisation might increase the numbers of proletarians and therefore the chances of Revolution, Witte's future was less certain. The revolution of 1905 seemed to be evidence of that and Stolypin returned to a policy of reform largely based on agriculture.

Conclusion. Return to the main point of the essay and your argument. Draw together each of the paragraph headings before summing up with a point which provides a short pithy answer to the question.

'What made Russia's problems insoluble was the Tsars determination to maintain the system of autocracy. Russians and non-Russians alike were regarded as a threat. Too often they resorted to repression rather than reform, and what little reform occurred was for the sole object of preserving their rule intact.'

Glossary

Ausgleich – Movement for the separation of the subject races of the Austrian Empire advocated by Magyars (Hungarians).

Bieno Rosso – A period of industrial unrest in Italy before the First World War.

bourgeois – Middle class, or the values of that class.

Copenhagen – Refers to a pre-emptive strike carried out by Nelson against the Danish fleet in Copenhagen during the Napoleonic Wars.

Coup d'état – Seizure of power.

Entente Cordiale – Settlement of differences. Specifically an agreement to end hostility between Britain and France in 1904.

Dreikaiserbund – Three Emperor's League (Austria, Russia, Germany).

Duma – A Russian parliament.

'Great Game' – Espionage carried out by Great Britain and Russia in the North West Frontier of India/Afghanistan.

Great Powers – Austro-Hungrian Empire, France, Great Britain, Prussia and Russia.

Italia Irredenta – Parts of Italy not yet under the Italian state government.

Lebensraum – 'Living space'.

jehad – A Muslim holy war.

Junkers – Prussian aristocrats.

Laissez-faire – An absence of state control or regulation.

Luddites – Machine wreckers in England in the early nineteenth century.

Mir – A Russian village commune.

nihilist – A person who rejects all religious and moral principles.

Protectionism – A system of tariffs designed to protect domestic industry from foreign competition.

Rapprochement – Reconciliation.

Realpolitik – Politics with a practical, rather than an ideological or moral, basis.

Revanche – Revenge.

Sammlungspolitik – 'Togetherness politics', political unity in Germany.

Serfdom – Akin to feudalism; peasants who were bound to serve their landlords in return for protection.

Soviet – Workers council, or, abbreviation for the Union of Soviet Socialist Republics.

Staatsfeinde – Enemies of the State. (Reichsfeinde – enemies of the Empire.)

Ukase – A Russian edict.

Weltpolitik – Expansion of German interests abroad.

Zemstvo – A provincial council in Russia.

Useful Web Sites

General sites
http://www.historytoday.com/article/
This site contains a wealth of material and reviews on recent books: ideal when tracking down new arguments and the ideas of certain authors. Book reviews can also be found at: *http://www.ihrinfo.ac.uk/ihr/reviews/revmnu.html*

A gateway to sites that are carefully selected by both Higher and Further education history specialists is at: *http://www.humbul.ac.uk*

Another recommended gateway is: *http://Britannica.com/bcom/history/0,5758,,00.html*

France
http://mars.acnet.wnec.edu/~grempel/courses/wc2/lectures/rev891.html
The origins of liberal democracy are explained here.

Germany
http://www.colby.edu/personal/rmscheck/Contents.html
This is a comprehensive site dedicated to all aspects of German history. Try starting with Bismarck.

Austria-Hungary
http://www.omnibusol.com/westernciv.html ('century before the Great War'). This site is a 'must visit' collection on the nineteenth century, including the concepts of nationalism and conservatism.

Russia
http://mars.acnet.wnec.edu/~grempel/courses/russia/lectures.html This is a lecture series by Professor Rempel which is very thorough.

http://history1900s.about.com/education/history1900s/msub15htm This is a helpful starting point for studies of the Russian Revolution, but also about the condition of the country at the turn of the century.

Great Britain
Aspects of British political, social, economic and cultural life can be found at:
http://www.indiana.edu/~victoria/other.html and also at:
http://landow.stg.brown.edu/victorian/victov.html

Italy

Links to the roots of fascism can be found at:

http://www.historytoday.com/historyreview/archives/96/fascism.html

International relations and the First World War

www.worldwar1.com is a fully comprehensive site on the causes and course of the war.

Bibliography and Further Reading

Barlett, C.J., Peace, *War and the European Powers, 1814–1914* (1996)

Chamberlain, M.E., *The Scramble for Africa* (1974)

Craig, Gordon, *Germany, 1866–1945* (1978)

Joll, James, *The Origins of the First World War* (1984)

Lowe, John, *Rivalry and Accord: International Relations, 1870–1914* (1990)

Martel, Gordon, *The Origins of the First World War* (1987)

Mason, John W., *The Dissolution of the Austro-Hungarian Empire, 1867–1918* (1985)

Pelling, Nick, *The Habsburg Empire* (1996)

Porter, Ian and Ian D. Armour, *Imperial Germany 1890–1918* (1991)

Randell, Keith, *France: The Third Republic, 1870–1914* (1986)

Robson, Mark, *Italy: Liberalism and Fascism 1870–1945* (1992)

Seaman, L.C.B., *From Vienna to Versailles* (1955)

Stiles, Andrina, *The Unification of Germany, 1815–1890* (1986)

Taylor, A.J.P., *The Struggle for Mastery in Europe* (1954)

Terraine, John, *The First World War* (1965)

Turner, L.C.F., *The Origins of the First World War* (1970)

Waldron, Peter, *The End of Imperial Russia 1855–1917* (1997)

Index

Aisne, 132
Alexander of Battenberg, 47–8
Alexander II, Tsar, 4, 21, 61–3, 65–7, 75
Alexander II, Tsar, 36, 67–8
alliance system, 112–113
Alsace Lorraine, 16, 18, 21, 22, 30, 37, 40, 112, 114
anti-clericalism, 18–20, 28
anti-Semitism, 19, 37, 39, 55, 67, 68, 73
Austria-Hungary, 3–4, 8, 11, 15, 28, 31, 39, 45, 50–2, 53–8, 91, 92, 113, 115–16, 118, 119–20, 123–4; (First World War), 133, 137, 138, 141

Balkans, 2, 11, 30, 31, 33, 40, 43, 44–9, 50, 57–8, 75, 119–20, 121–3
Balkan Wars, 100, 150
Berlin, Conference (1884), 103–114
Berlin, Congress of (1878), 31, 46, 74
Bethmann-Hollweg, Chancellor, 39–40, 124–5, 140
Bismarck, Prince Otto von, 3, 15, 25–34, 49, 110
Black Hand, 121
Bosnia, 45, 113 115, 116
Boulanger Affair, 18–19, 48
British Empire, 78, 80 see also imperialism
Brusilov Offensive, 141
Bulgaria, 32, 44–5, 46, 47–9, 51, 119–20, 138
Bülow, Chancellor, 37, 117

capitalism, see industrialisation
Caporetto, 137
Caprivi, Chancellor, 37
Catholic Centre Party, 27–9
Catholic Church, 3, 18, 28, 67, 93–4
China, 12, 36, 97, 98, 106–7, 112

Commune, The, 16, 23

democracy, 2, 3, 14, 36, 73, 78–9, 89–90, 145, 149
Denmark, 30
Dreikaiserbund, 31–2, 45, 74
Dreyfus Case, 19, 23
Dual Alliance, 31–2
Dual Monarchy, see Austria Hungary

Egypt, 11, 44, 47, 99, 100–102, 115
Emancipation of the Serfs, 4, 61–2, 70

Ferdinand, Archduke Franz, 58, 121
Finland, 67, 73
France, 2, 7, 8, 12, 14–24, 25, 28, 32, 39, 44, 47, 74, 98–100, 103–104, 107, 113, 115, 117, 123, 146; (First World War), 128, 129, 130–1, 137, 141
Franz-Josef, Emperor, 31, 55
free trade, 7, 27, 29, 77

Germany, 12, 25–41, 45, 83, 91, 99-100, 103, 108, 113–14, 115–8, 123, 124–5, 146; (First World War), 127–33, 135, 137–8, 141
Great Game, 105
Great War, 12, 94, 127–42, 150
Greece, 11, 43, 47, 49, 112, 119–20
Guesde, Jules, 21

Hague, Conventions, 130
Hindenburg, Paul von, 132–3, 140
Hungary, see Austria-Hungary

imperialism, 5, 22, 91, 96–110, 114, 136, 146, 149
industrialisation, 2, 5–7, 9, 29, 38, 68–9, 77, 97, 118, 145

inventions, 110, 112, 140, 147–8
Ireland, 77, 80, 81
Islam, 35, 43, 102, 109, 120, 142
Italia Irredenta, 90–1, 135
Italy, 4, 8, 22–23, 49, 86–94, 99–100,
    104; (First World War), 134–5

Japan, 40, 72, 74, 83, 106, 112, 114
July Crisis, 120

Kulturkampf, 28, 31

Lenin, V.I., 71, 146
liberalism, 2, 10, 77, 79, 81, 136, 144

Magyarisation, 54, 56–7, 121
March Offensive, 1918, 138–140
Marx, Karl and Marxism, 24, 30, 66,
    71, 75, 124, 147
Mediterranean Agreements, 83, 92
militarism, 39, 114, 145
Morocco, 41, 92, 115, 116–17

Napoleon III, 2–3, 14–15, 25
nationalism, 1, 3, 5, 10, 18, 55, 101, 107,
    114, 141, 145
Nicholas, II, Tsar, 36, 75

Orthodox Church, 43, 61
Ottoman Empire, 1, 3, 43–51, 99, 109,
    119; (First World War), 134–5

Panama Canal, 19
Pan-Slavism, 44–5, 55
Papacy and Popes, 19, 28, 86, 88, 90,
    93–4
Poland, 64–5, 74
Portugal, 101, 103–104
Prussia, 7–8, 12, 15, 27, 88

Ralliement, 93
Reichstag (Germany), 27, 31, 36, 40, 49,
    139; (Austrian), 56
Reinsurance Treaty, 31, 33
Revanche, 18, 33

revolution, 9, 38, 65–6, 71, 72, 90, 141
Romania, 11, 43, 47, 57, 72
Russia, 4, 7–8, 21–22, 31–3, 35–6, 37,
    40, (1877) 45–6; (1885) 47–9, 50;
    (post 1885) 60–75, 99, 105–106, 113,
    118, 120, 122; (First World War),
    127, 128, 131, 137, 138–9, 140–41
Russification, 67
Russo-Japanese War, 72, 74, 107, 115,
    116

San Stefano, 46
Schlieffen Plan, 39, 118, 127, 128, 139
scramble for Africa, 100–105
Serbia, 11, 32, 43, 45, 47, 51, 52, 57,
    113, 116, 118, 119–20, 121–2; (First
    World War), 134
socialism, 9, 10, 18, 21, 29–30, 37–8, 68,
    72, 89, 137
Social Darwinism, 98, 114, 146
Social Revolutionaries, 70, 73
Somme, 130–1
Soviets, 73, 75, 139, 140
Stolypin, Piotyr, 70, 73
Suez Canal, 101–2, 134

Tannenburg, 133
Thiers, Adolphe, 16, 23
Transformismo, 89–90

United States of America, 7, 29, 62, 69,
    74–5, 91, 97, 101, 112, 141, 144

Verdun, 127, 130–1

Weltpolitik, 34, 35
Wilhelm II, Kaiser, 34–8, 39, 114, 116,
    119, 123–5, 127, 139, 141
Witte, Sergei, 68–70

Young Turks, 45, 51, 120
Ypres, 128

Zabern Affair, 39